A
Passion
for
His
Presence

by

LaMar Boschman

Revival Press
Worship and Praise Division
of
Destiny Image Publishers
P.O. Box 310
Shippensburg, PA 17257-0310

ISBN 1-56043-704-9

Printed in the United States of America
For Worldwide Distribution

First Printing: 1992
Second Printing: 1994

Dedication

To my pastor, Glen Roachelle and his wife, Roberta, who have been a tremendous gift to us from the Lord. Their counsel and love have been a covering for my wife, Teresa, myself, and our two sons, Jonathan and Jordan.

Table of Contents

Author's Preface
Introduction

Manifest Presence as Light, His Manifest Presence
as a Sound From Heaven and as Tongues of Fire)

Author's Preface

This book has come about through two years of God's dealings with me. In many ways, this has been one of the most difficult periods of my life, yet it has also been one of the most fruitful periods of my life. With God's help, I have been stripped of annoying distractions that sapped my strength. This resulted in an opportunity to simply sit at the Lord's feet and focus on Him.

With joy and confidence I can declare that I now know what the Lord expects of me as we prepare for the next millennium. It is from this perspective that I write for the spiritual refreshment of others. May this book call each of those who read it to new levels in their relationship with the Lord and help them to find the keys to *the secret place of the Most High.*

Introduction

The presence of God can be both a very comforting and a very terrible force. It can be a sanctuary of intimate communion, bringing a sense of great peace and comfort. At the same time, it can exert a force that actually slays multitudes. On occasion, in biblical times, the presence of the Lord destroyed entire armies, caused large numbers of men to go blind and whole nations to become ill.

On one such occasion, an entire Assyrian army of one hundred and eighty-five thousand men was destroyed in one night, as God moved by His awesome presence among them. The next morning, only dead corpses remained. The presence of God killed Egyptian and Hebrew first-born one unforgettable dark night in Egypt. Only those who had blood sprinkled on their door posts escaped.

The Bible says:

> *As wax melts before the fire, so let the wicked perish at the presence of God. But let the righteous be glad; let them rejoice before God; Yes, let them rejoice exceedingly.*   Psalms 68:2-3

What a difference there is in the effect God's presence has on people! In some, it causes great joy, while — in others — it causes great sorrow. There is a direct connection between the relationship people have with the Lord and how His presence affects them.

God's presence can bring terror to those who do not love and serve Him. To those of us who do love Him, He calls — to come into His presence joyfully and expectantly.

God's presence, how we come into His presence, and what happens to us when we come into His presence are the subjects of this book, one that I believe will change your life forever. Through it, you can learn to know God's presence in your daily life — in your home, in your school or in your office — not just in your church building. In these pages, we will learn how to enter into God's presence at any time and in any place. And learning the secrets of entering God's presence anywhere and at any time will speed us on our way toward our ultimate goal as believers — living in His presence.

LaMar Boschman

Chapter 1

The Omnipresence of God

Can any hide himself in secret places, that I shall not see him? saith the Lord. Do not I fill heaven and earth? saith the Lord. Jeremiah 23:24 (KJV)

During certain times in history God's presence was manifested in unusual ways. The revealing of His presence produced strange phenomena. On one such occasion the Bible says that hills collapsed or fell down as God's presence passed by them.

> *The hills melted like wax at the presence of the Lord, at the presence of the Lord of the whole earth.*
>
> Psalms 97:5

On another occasion nature sang out as the presence of the Lord was manifested.

> *Then shall the trees of the wood sing out at the presence of the Lord, because he cometh to judge the earth.*
>   1 Chronicles 16:33 (KJV)

Sometimes the presence of the Lord was not associated with pleasantness, but with His wrath. Jeremiah gives us an example:

> *I beheld, and, lo, the fruitful place was a wilderness, and all the cities thereof were broken down at the presence of the Lord, and by his fierce anger.*
>   Jeremiah 4:26 (KJV)

But whether or not there is any indication of His presence, God is present everywhere. Nothing can change that fact. He is not always seen or felt or heard or observed, but He is always there. Our God is omnipresent — present everywhere at once.

Some might misinterpret God's statement that He fills heaven and earth to mean that His authority is over all, much as an earthly ruler might claim authority over his entire kingdom. An earthly king may indeed have authority and power over all his empire; but he can, in no way, fill all the cities and countryside of his domain — as does our God.

God is everywhere. No place can be deprived of His presence. Since He fills everything, no place can be without Him. God is in every city, in every state, in every street, in every house, in every field, in every forest, and on every mountain. He is so immense that He fills everything.

The Immensity of His Presence

God is present in all places. His presence is everywhere always. He is as immense as He is eternal. His indivisible existence reaches through all time and through all places.

As all times are a moment to His eternity, so all places are a pinpoint to His massive essence. As God is larger than all time, so He is more vast than all places. Our God is immense.

> *Behold, the nations are as a drop in a bucket,*
> *And are counted as the small dust on the balance;*
> *Look, He lifts up the isles as a very little thing.*
> Isaiah 40:15

This immensity is not easily understood. If a man were set in the highest heavens, he would not be nearer to God than if he were in the center of the earth. You cannot be nearer to God or further from God, no matter where you are; for He is everywhere. His presence is immense.

The presence of God in the world is like the presence of the soul in the body. The soul is essentially in every part of man's small world. The soul animates every member of the body by its presence, though it does not effect the same operation in every part.

The world is less to God than the body of a man is to his soul. The world needs the presence of God more than the body needs the presence of the soul. Our God is immense.

David was aware of the fact that he could never escape the immensity of God's presence. He said:

Where can I go from Your Spirit?
Or where can I flee from Your presence?
If I ascend into heaven, You are there;
If I make my bed in hell, behold, You are there.
If I take the wings of the morning,
And dwell in the uttermost parts of the sea, Even there
Your hand shall lead me,
And Your right hand shall hold me.

Psalms 139:7-10

Where indeed? God is always everywhere. In heaven, God is; in hell, God is; in the earth, God is. He is not just "in" heaven or "in" hell or "in" the earth. He is everywhere. He fills heaven and earth. He fills, totally encompasses, both outwardly and inwardly, the earth and the expanse of all the heavens.

He is present by His glory in heaven, comforting the saints who have gone before us; and He is present by His wrath in hell, meting out punishment to the damned. In heaven, He is spreading His love as a blanket. In hell, He is administering justice as only He can. He is always present everywhere.

He is in all places present with all creatures, seen and unseen, terrestrial and celestial. He can be your constant companion and, at the same time, be the constant companion of everyone else who loves Him.

You cannot leave His omnipresence nor return to His omnipresence. He is always everywhere, like the air around us. But He is so much greater than the air around us; for He is also present in the farthest extremities of space and beyond.

Since God is in heaven, He is with all the angels. He is with all the cherubs, and all the seraphim. Since He is in hell, He is with all the damned. He is present with all the spirits that roam the surface of the earth, hoping to influence (or enter and dwell in) beasts or men.

He is present with the fallen angels and principalities that rule in the heavens over the cities and municipalities of the world. He is just as much present with the kingdom of darkness and all its principles as He is with all the redeemed who live in the Kingdom of Light. The immensity of God's presence is such that He is with the darkest devils, just as He is with the brightest angels.

He is with the lowly dust, just as He is with the sparkling sun. He is equally present with the damned and the blessed. He is equally present with the good and the bad. He is so immense that nothing and nobody is removed from or outside of His presence. He covers all and dwells within all.

Some have limited God's presence to heaven. Consequently they think that when they get to heaven they will be closer to Him. Considering His omnipresence, however, that concept cannot possibly be correct. We can never be nearer or further from God's presence. We can neither leave His presence nor enter into it. That particular dimension of God's presence is always (at all times) everywhere (in all places). He fills *"heaven and earth"* — equally.

When we enter heaven, we will not enter God's presence (in this sense). His omnipresence is as real here on earth as it is in heaven. He is everywhere and fills everything.

As David discovered, if we could sprout wings and fly to the farthest reaches of the universe in a moments time, we would find that God's presence was there before us. What a thought! The fastest wings cannot go ahead of God's presence. He is already everywhere, and He is always everywhere.

God is infinite in His being, so His presence is infinite. It has no beginning, and it has no end. He encompasses all and is encompassed by none. He fills all and is comprehended by none.

The Creator contains the world, yet the world does not contain the Creator. If all things live and move in Him, then He is present with everything that has life and motion. Whatever lives and moves, lives and moves in Him. This is the "bigness" of the essence of our God.

The "bigness" of God is incomprehensible to the finite mind. The fact that He is so immense and that He fills everything makes it impossible for us to understand Him in His entirety. There is nothing with which to compare Him and no words to adequately describe Him.

If we cannot conceive of the vastness and glory of the heavens, how much less can we conceive of the greatness of God? He fills all the vastness of the universe, yet it is too small to contain Him. What a great God we serve!

No creature can exclude His presence. Not only is He *near* everyone and everything, He is *in* everyone and everything. The Apostle Paul stated it aptly in his discourse on Mars Hill:

For in Him we live, and move, and have our being.
                                        Acts 17:28 (KJV)

He is not absent from anyone or anything. He is so much present that He is more important to life than the air we breathe. He is nearer to us than our muscles are to our bones. We do not live and move "by Him"; we live and move "*in Him.*"

The Boundlessness of His Presence

God's presence is so immense that no boundaries can be ascribed to it. He simply has no limits. God is so much a part of everything that His essence is mixed with that of every creature, yet He remains distinct and apart from the essence of any of His created beings.

A body or a spirit, because it is finite, can only fill one space at a time; God, because He is infinite, fills every space, yet is not contained by them all. He is from the heights of the heavens to the very depths of the heavens. He is in every point of the earth, and in the whole circle of it, yet not limited by it. He extends far beyond.

God is present beyond all places. He is within and above all places, even if there are an infinite number of worlds. He is before and beyond all time, so He is above and beyond all places. Being from eternity before any real time, He also must be without as well as within any real space.

If the world confined God, He would have no greater essence than that which the limited world permitted Him. It is not so. If a moment cannot be imagined separate from eternity, then a space cannot be imagined where God is not present. God cannot be contained in the earth or in the heavens.

> *"But will God indeed dwell on the earth? Behold,*
> *heaven and the heaven of heavens cannot contain*
> *You."*   1 Kings 8:27

These are the words of the great King Solomon. As he considered the immensity of God's essence, he was overwhelmed. Why, then, did he order a temple built for God — when the *heaven of heavens* cannot contain an essence so immense? God's greatness extends far beyond heaven.

If God can create innumerable worlds, He can be in innumerable spaces. If He has enough power to make more worlds, He has enough essence to fill them. He cannot be confined to what He has already created. Innumerable worlds would not be sufficient to contain Him.

God is a place only to Himself. He that was before the worlds and before specific places, was to Himself a world and a place. The worlds cannot contain Him for He was contained by nothing before He created the worlds. So great is our God!

If there were spaces between the worlds, God would not only fill the worlds and beyond but also would fill all the dimensions between them. God fills all with His presence.

> *The heaven is my throne, and the earth is my footstool.*
> Isaiah 66:1 (KJV)

He is in heaven and earth at the same time, using heaven as a man might sit upon his throne and the earth as a man might rest his feet on a footstool. He fills all the space between heaven and earth, as well. Some have said that this example speaks only of God's power or royalty. I believe that it speaks of His awesome essence.

If God has an infinite essence, then He has an infinite presence. An infinite essence cannot be contained in a finite place, for He is not limited by time or place. He is present absolutely everywhere and absolutely always. The same cannot be said of other gods:

Throughout history, the gods of the heathen were believed to have a particular dominion. They were present in one place. These gods were limited by certain territories or borders.

The root meaning of our word *principality* is *the area of government given to a prince.* It is for this reason that many nations of the world and many cities have their own unique personality. They each have a different principality. Each principality has a set boundary or limit to the dominion of their spiritual government, the demons or gods which rule over them.

When I was in Haiti, I learned how real voodoo gods were to those who worship them. I could hear the people beating their drums and calling on the voodoo spirits far into the night. Each voodoo god is believed to be unique, and each is territorial, limited to one particular area.

The American Indians held certain places to be more sacred than others because they believed that one of their gods dwelt in that particular spot.

Even the Jews thought that God was confined to heaven. They made their sacrifices on the highest available mountain, trusting that the smoke from the sacrifice would ascend to heaven. They thought that God could more easily hear their praises when they stood on a high place.

Some Christians have a very similar concept. They limit God to a building (a cathedral, for example) or to a particular liturgy. Most Christians feel closer to God in a building dedicated to worship. While it may be true that God manifests His presence more in places dedicated to worship, it is also true that He is everywhere. He is not more present in a church or on top of a mountain than He is in any other place. He is everywhere always.

God is not more present in the church than He is in your home. Ours is not a God that dwells in temples made with hands. It is true that He dwells in His people in a special way and that, wherever His people can be found, He is there. But He is not limited by our faith in Him. He is everywhere always.

God is present in the church. He is present in the grocery store. He is in your car. He is in your home. He is in the office. He is in the park. He is present everywhere. No boundaries can be ascribed to Him.

When you leave the sanctuary of your local church and pass through the foyer and out into the street, you have not left the omnipresence of God. He is in every street, always.

If His presence were to be limited to heaven, He could not fill heaven and earth. To say God is more present in heaven is to limit Him. As we are free to move about from room to room, God can move about from one dimension to another; for He fills them all. Our concept of God does not limit Him. He is eternally limitless and boundless.

How could God, Who was so immense even before He created the world, confine Himself to the limits of that which He brought into existence? How could He be less after His creation than He was before? He, Who is eternal in duration, is also boundless in His presence. The same facts that determine Him to be eternal determine Him to be limitless. What a wonderful God we serve!

Not only is God's presence unlimited by place; He is also unlimited by time. Our heavenly Father inhabits eternity. He dwells in the infinite past, in the present, and also in the future. He has always been present — without bounds or restrictions of time.

> *For thus says the High and Lofty One*
> *Who inhabits eternity, whose name is holy.*
> Isaiah 57:15

God cannot be measured or limited by time. The boundlessness of His presences includes time. Because He is present everywhere to maintain and to create, He can do it immediately. He is so perfect that He can work all things instantly. He knows all things immediately because He is present everywhere, so He can act immediately. Because He is always present with all things, there need be no delay.

God does not require time to gather His tools. He is never delayed by the need to travel. It takes Him no time at all to identify the problem and to begin the process of repair. He is perfectly equipped, everywhere present and all knowing. Nothing escapes His eye. What a perfect God!

The Indivisibility of His Presence

God's presence is unlike the presence of matter, as we know it. If a vessel is filled with a liquid, one part of the liquid fills one part of the vessel and another part of the liquid fills another part of the vessel. But it is not a "part" of God which fills one place and another "part" of God which fills another place. All of God is everywhere, in everything, always.

The Creator fills His creation. God fills the entirety of heaven and earth. There is no spot that does not contain Him. The whole of God completely fills heaven, and the whole of God completely fills the earth. God is everywhere present in heaven and everywhere present in the earth.

The essential presence of God is never divided. He fills heaven and earth, not part of Him fills heaven and part of Him fills earth. All of Him fills the one place as well as the other. One part of His essence is not in one place, while another part of His essence is in another place. He is undivided, and He is everywhere.

Although we divide eternity into past, present and future, it is, in reality, one indivisible point. God is not divided. It is impossible for one part of His essence to be separable from another. Anything that has parts is finite. God is infinite, therefore there are no parts to His essence.

Parts signify composition. God has no parts. He is unique. He is all and in all. We can say that God is *here*. We can say that God is *there*. We cannot say that part of God is here or that part of God is there. All of God is here and all of God is there. He is altogether everywhere, not by fragments or parts, but in His entirety. This is the mystery of the immensity of our God.

The essential presence of God cannot be multiplied, for that which is infinite cannot become larger. God cannot multiply Himself, for He is as large as He can possibly be. He cannot be more powerful, for He is already ALL powerful. He cannot be present in more places, for He is already present everywhere. He cannot gain more knowledge and wisdom for He already has ALL knowledge and wisdom.

A piece of gold can be stretched or beaten out to cover a larger area. But God's basic essence cannot be extended. If God created a million worlds, He would be in them all — not by stretching Himself, but by the infiniteness of His being; not by an extension of His being, but by His original essence.

The Immutability of His Presence

God does not change. He is unchangeable and unchanging.

> *The heavens are the work of Your hands.*
> *They will perish, but You will endure;*
> *Yes, all of them will grow old like a garment;*
> *Like a cloak You will change them,*
> *And they will be changed.*
> *But You are the same,*
> *And Your years will have no end.*
>
> Psalms 102:25-27

God is Spirit (John 4:24) and is in all time, past, present and future, and in all places the same. His presence is constant, unwavering, and totally stable. He said so, Himself.

> *"For I am the Lord, I do not change."*
>
>   Malachi 3:6

Change is not always good and not always bad. Some changes are for the better, while others are for the worse. But God can neither be any better, nor any worse. There is nothing about Him to change. He is perfect and maintains that perfect state constantly.

> *Every good and every perfect gift is from above, and comes down from the Father of lights, with whom there is no variation, or shadow of turning.*
>
>   James 1:17

Because God is always the same, His omnipresence (His all-presence) is the same. It is never altered. The omnipresence of God is the same today as it was at the time when Paul wrote his letter to the Romans, or the time when Moses led the children of Israel through the wilderness. It is even the same as it was during the time of the creation.

God's presence is perfect and, therefore, constant, never diminishing or dissipating. It needs no maintenance. He has always been solidly present, and He always will be. Nothing can change that fact.

Praise our God!

The Omniscience of His Presence

God is immense. He is everywhere. He fills everything. He is in the deepest cells of every creature. He is present on every star of every galaxy in the universe. He is present in everything and in every place, both in the heavens and on earth. That is why God knows everything, another of His incomprehensible attributes.

God knows everything because He is present with everything. Because His presence is infinite, He cannot be distant from anything, and nothing can be far from His sight. He sees everything and knows everything because everything is near Him.

We humans know things in one of two ways. Either information is conveyed to us, or we must be present to acquire the information through our senses. God does not have these limitations. Because He is everywhere, both within and without all the extremities of the farthest and nearest reaches of heaven and the earth, and because He fills everything, He knows everything.

The Potency of His Presence

The presence of God is a potent force. The eternal God, who has infinite goodness, wisdom and power, and Who is present everywhere always, is never without exercise of those attributes. Because He is everywhere, with everything He created, He is not without concern for all those things. God is never negligent. He is constantly vigilant.

Because He is near, He is aware of every need and, therefore, efficient in His caring. He is not everywhere just to be everywhere. He is everywhere to act. And He does act. Wherever His presence is, power and virtue are dispensed. The Creator is omnipotent, and that omnipotence is not without operation. His presence is potent.

God governs because He is present with all things. He governs by His presence what He made by His power. His presence and His power are together to preserve the created, as His presence and power were together when He first created everything. Every creature has the mark of the Creator upon it, and His presence is necessary to keep that impression valid.

Where God works by His power, He is present. His power and His presence cannot be separated. His power cannot be anywhere that His presence is not. For the power of God to act, He must be present.

Because His presence is unlimited, His power is unlimited. As His presence cannot be confined, His power cannot be confined. He is *almighty*.

Fifty six times the Bible uses the word *almighty*. *Almighty*, however, is only used in reference to God. He is the *Almighty*. He is all powerful. There is nothing that He cannot do. There is no limit to the energy of His presence. It takes Him no more energy to create a universe than it does to make a flower grow. He can do one thing as easily as He can do another. He does everything easily, without dissipating His strength. He never tires.

> *The Everlasting God, the Lord, the Creator of the ends of the earth neither faints nor is weary.*
>
> Isaiah 40:28

God's presence never needs to be replenished; for it never runs out. He never gets tired, and He never faints.

There are two areas in which the power of His presence can be seen most clearly. One is in His ability to create something out of nothing. The marvel of creation is, therefore, one of the most potent witnesses to the power of His presence.

> *By the word of the Lord the heavens were made;*
> *And all the hosts of them by the breath of His mouth.*
> *For He spoke, and it was done;*
> *He commanded, and it stood fast.*
>
> Psalms 33:6 & 9

Perhaps we cannot witness the creation. But the ability of our God to redeem the lost speaks just as forcefully of His "almightiness" as does the creation. And we can all witness this marvel.

God is present with all men to draw them to Himself. His power in redemption is more awesome than it was in creation. In creation, there was no opposition, no devil to subdue, no death to be conquered, no sin to be pardoned, no hell to be shut, and no cross to be suffered.

The mystery of the Gospel is the good news that all this has been successfully dealt with — because God, is and because His presence is potent. Our God is the Almighty. Nothing is too hard for Him.

His presence is not less than His power, and His power is not less than His presence. The two cannot be separated. Wherever He exerts His power, there He is. Wherever He displays His might, He is present. If He were not present,

His power could not be there either. And where He is, His power is evidenced.

Before the world was made, He had power to make it and to hang it in space. He was there. He was present, therefore His power acted.

Power is synonymous with the presence of God. The Bible speaks of *"the Son of Man sitting on the right hand of Power*, (Mark 14:62) that is, at the right hand of God. God and power are so inseparable that they are interchangeable. His presence brings the demonstration of His power.

The Purity of His Presence

His immense and potent presence is pure, unmixed with anything else. Although He *fills* heaven and earth, He is not *mixed* with heaven and earth. Although He is *in* all creation, His presence is not mixed with creation. It remains pure and entire.

A sponge at the bottom of the ocean is encompassed by the sea, filled by the sea water, and is moving in and with the sea. The sponge, however, still retains its own nature. God's essence does not mix with anything. It is pure.

The light of the sun is present with the air but does not mix with it. The light remains light, and the air remains air. As our planet turns on its axis, the light of the sun is diffused through all the earth. That sunlight pierces transparent objects, yet it does not mix with them. The light remains light, and the transparent object remains intact and unmixed with the light. The object may have been infused with light, but it is not light.

Although God is present in all things, He is not formally one with those things in the sense of losing His essence in them. He remains God; and they remain things.

God is not everywhere by conjunction, composition or mixture with anything, either on earth or in heaven. His essence touches everything; yet it is in conjunction with nothing. The finite and the infinite cannot be joined. Nothing becomes God simply because it moves in Him. Fish move about in the sea, but a fish is not the sea. A fish is a fish, and the sea is the sea.

Just because God is in everything, everything is not to be worshiped — as some have taught. Only God is to be worshiped. Everything else derives its life from Him. Although He is in everything, and everything is in Him, He is still God. He is not mixed with that which He indwells.

Someone who worships the created is not worshiping the Creator. The substance of the created and the substance of the Creator are separate. Because Christ is in me does not mean that I should be worshiped. I am not Christ, and Christ is not me — although He abides in me, and I abide in Him.

In the same way, although God is with everything and in everything, He is not defiled by anything. Because His essence is not mixed with anything, it cannot be defiled. Being with the vilest creature cannot defile the presence of God.

He created everything. Could He be more defiled by being with something than by creating it in the first place? Are God's eyes defiled by seeing something imperfect, deteriorated or rotten? What could be more vile than the grave or hell? Yet He is there — as we have seen.

According to the book of Job, Satan appeared before God and spoke with Him (Job 1:7). Could God have been defiled or could He have contracted some impurity through association with that filthy spirit? No! God's purity stands in the midst of filthiness. He is heaven to Himself in the midst of hell. God can be present with devils or with wicked men and can witness the grossest sins imaginable and still not be affected by what He sees.

An angel appeared to Daniel in the lion's den. Yet the angel was not stained by the experience of imprisonment, defiled by the stench of the animal pit, or torn apart by the sharp teeth and claws of the beasts. In the same way, God is not affected by the evil and rottenness He might witness. He cannot be defiled. His presence is pure.

It is hard for us to imagine that God could be present with us when we commit some secret sin. Yet He is. He is present when the adulterer commits his evil act. Yet our God is not defiled.

The knowledge of God's presence should cause us to stop sinning. He is present everywhere. He sees everything that we do. He overhears everything that we say. He is conscious of all the affairs of men. Nothing is done in secret.

Most of us, however, instead of acknowledging God's presence and refraining from sin, try to deny to ourselves and others that He is actually there and that He actually witnesses all our deeds. How small our impression of the God of the universe must be, to think that He does not see and know!

He sees all. He knows all. Yet He is defiled by nothing. His presence is pure.

The Effectiveness of His Presence

God is present everywhere by His authority: all things are subject to Him. He is present everywhere by His power: all things are sustained by Him. He is present everywhere by His knowledge: all things are naked before Him. He is providentially present with all: His power extends to the lowest of His creatures; and His knowledge pierces everything.

All things in the world were created by Him, so everything is preserved by Him, as well. Preservation is not completely distinct from creation, and God was present when He created everything; therefore, it is understandable that He should be present with everything while He preserves it. David said:

> *You preserve man and beast.*   Psalms 36:6

The writer of Hebrews declares that God upholds all things *"by the word of His power"* (Hebrews 1:3). His virtue sustains every living creature to prevent it from falling back into that nothingness from which it originally came. It was first elevated by the power of God and must now be maintained by that same power. He is present with everything to maintain it, to guard it, to watch over it and to guide its progress.

What wonderful peace and security that gives the created! We should rejoice in that fact. He is close to us to keep us. Nothing can deter His preserving presence.

Our God manages everything. He is the gardener who never leaves the garden for a moment. He is present with every plant and knows everything there is to know about each. Nothing escapes His watchful eye.

If He can create all things, He can restore all things. And no damage is too difficult for Him to repair. He can restore our broken relationships. Nothing is impossible with God.

God preserves all because He is in all. He works in everything, and everything lives and works in Him. If something lives, it is because God gives it life. Nothing lives apart from Him. He is life. If something moves, it is because God gives it motion. Anything and everything that exists does so because God gives it existence. If God withdraws Himself, everything ceases to exist. Nothing can exist apart from him. His presence created everything, and His presence preserves everything.

God is the center of all molecular structure. All things are comprised of Him. He holds everything together and gives everything form and substance. As His essential presence was the foundation of the first existence of things by creation, so it is the foundation of the continued existence of everything created.

In the beginning, He measured the waters of the earth in the hollow of His hand, stretched the heavens out from the land, measured the dust of the earth in a thimble, and weighed the mountains and hills on a scale. God's power and majesty are set forth in the creation and preservation of all living things, for it is achieved only by His presence.

The Objectivity of His Presence

Aside from God's effective presence to preserve all life, there exists also His objective presence. He offers Himself to His creatures to be known and loved by them. He makes Himself available for a personal relationship. He reveals Himself through supernatural means, causing a miracle to happen for which there is no reasonable explanation, except that GOD is present and seeks to be acknowledged.

Some call these events "fate," or "fortune," or "luck," or "mother nature." They are manifestations of the omnipresence of a preserving and loving Father, whose presence is everywhere to influence the course of the lives of men and women.

As we catch glimpses of God's handiwork, we are made to realize that there is genius behind everything that exists. It did not just happen. It did not just accidentally fall into place. Everything that exists could not have been made by anyone other than our great God.

In recent years, God has permitted us to delve more deeply into molecular structure and to catch a glimmer of the power that holds all things together.

He has permitted us to look further into space, through our spacecraft, satellites and super-telescopes, giving us a window to the heavens. We have been permitted to look beyond the milky way galaxy and to discover what appear to be millions of other galaxies — each larger than our own.

While we have been busy with all of this and, at the same time, trying to ignore God and declare that He doesn't even exist, He just keeps smiling and manifesting His presence to us.

Men have developed elaborate theories of creation to deny God His glory. But that doesn't change Him. The Father of Life is still present, still preserving creation, still holding everything together by His power. Even when men curse Him, He is still there in all the cells of their being. He never ceases to exert His influence over His creation.

The Tangibleness of His Presence

God's presence everywhere is so real that it can be felt. It is evident to our senses.

The sun, although it stands at such a great distance from the earth, makes its presence felt on the earth in a very real way. The light of the sun affects the chemical makeup of the earth's vegetation. Yet the influence of the sun is not worthy to ever be compared with the influence of God's presence on every living thing.

God is intensely intimate with every living thing. Not even a small particle of matter exists which does not bear the marks of His power and goodness. His preserving goodness attends everything and is more swift in its influence than the speed of light from the sun, because He is right there with everything and in everything. Such is the excellency of His presence!

Have you ever wondered why people swear by the name of Jesus Christ or by God, our heavenly Father? They don't say, *"Allah damn"* or *"Buddha damn."* They instinctively recognize the existence of a higher power and use His name. They may even formally deny Him, yet they instinctively sense His presence. It is tangible.

When people are involved in an accident and are hurt or dying, they don't call out to Mohammed or Allah; they call out to the living God. Eternity is stamped on their hearts, and they can sense that God is both real and present. This leaves them *"without excuse."*

> *For the wrath of God is revealed from heaven against all ungodliness and unrighteousness of men, who suppress the truth in unrighteousness, because what may be known of God is manifest in them, for God has shown it to them. For since the creation of the world His invisible attributes are clearly seen, being understood by the things that are made, even His eternal power and Godhead, so that they are without excuse.*
> Romans 1:18-20

God can be seen in nature. Every majestic mountain, the vast seas, and all the amazing creatures in them testify of His greatness. The sense of the finger of God upon creation is evident to anyone willing to recognize it.

Paul encountered the reality of this when he was in ancient Athens, a city full of very religious people who constantly wanted either to tell or to be told some new truth.

> *Then Paul stood in the midst of the Areopagus and said, "Men of Athens, I perceive that in all things you are very religious; for as I was passing through and considering the objects of your worship, I even found an altar with this inscription: TO THE UNKNOWN GOD."*
> Acts 17:22-23

The Athenians, with all their created gods, instinctively knew that there was still another God, one who was different than all others, real and most supreme. Given the opportunity, Paul spoke of Him. He told them:

> *"He has made from one blood every nation of men to dwell on all the face of the earth, and has determined their preappointed times, and the boundaries of their habitation, so that they should seek the Lord, in the hope that they might grope for Him and find Him, though He is not far from each one of us."*
>
> Acts 17:26-27

God is real, and His reality can be sensed by the most pagan of men. It is tangible.

The fact of the objectivity of God's presence and the tangibleness of His presence leads us to another dimension of His presence, one into which we can enter and from which we can depart.

> *These shall be punished with everlasting destruction from the presence of the Lord and from the glory of His power,*   2 Thessalonians 1:9

When people are sentenced to *"everlasting destruction"* in hell, they are expelled from the presence of God. Is it possible that being cast out of His presence is the real punishment? Those who are no longer covered by the preserving *"glory of His power"* experience eternal destruction.

It is possible to be in the presence of God and not know it, not feel it. In the same way, it is possible to be banished from the presence of God. Let us now examine the manifestation of God's presence.

Chapter 2

The Manifestation of His Presence

And the Lord spoke unto Moses face to face, as a man speaks to his friend.   Exodus 33:11 (KJV)

Ever since the creation of man, God has revealed Himself to mankind in unusual and diverse ways. He has a desire to show Himself to people. He is a relational God and wants to be near those He created. That is why He reveals Himself to us as a Father. It has always been His desire to be close to man and to have man close to Him. He wants us to know Him. His heart is to disclose Himself to those He loves.

This brings us to another dimension of God's presence. Because it can be sensed, it is sometimes called His *felt* presence. Others call it His *revealed* presence. It is, simply, the *manifestation* of God's presence.

God is present everywhere. However, He does not always choose to reveal His presence. When He does choose to reveal Himself to us, He sometimes does it in unusual ways. He allows us to sense His presence. Usually we cannot see Him or hear Him or even feel Him (in the natural sense), yet we definitely know that He is present.

To those of us who know Him, knowing that we are in the presence of the Lord of our lives and the Lover of our souls creates a very deep excitement. Nothing could be more wonderful for us.

The Hebrew word for *presence,* used in Psalms 100:2 (*"Come before His presence with singing"*), means *before, at, or to the face of (in the sense of, in full view of, under the eye of, or at the disposal of).* This is not the omnipresence of God, in which everyone is technically in the presence of God. This speaks of a much closer and intimate sense of being before or in front of Him, having His full attention.

God is not calling us to just be where He is. He is calling us to come before His face, into His full view, under His loving gaze. He longs to look full into our eyes. What He desires is not a passing glance or a fleeting sight, but an intense stare.

When someone is staring at you from across a crowded room, it is amazing how quickly you notice it. There is an uncanny awareness that someone's eyes are on you, although you sometimes cannot immediately locate who it is who is staring at you.

The eyes of the Lord are upon us. He longs to catch our eye. He longs to draw our attention to Him, and to draw us to Him — so near that we are not only in front of Him, where He can look fully into our eyes, but right up "in His face." To Him, looking from across the room is not enough. He wants to be right there next to you. This is what it means to be *"in His presence."*

There is a phrase that some people use these days when they don't want someone to "hassle" them or to get too close to them. They want to be left alone. They say, *"Get out of my face."* God's heart is just the opposite. He doesn't want to be left alone. You are no problem to Him. He says, *"Get into My face. Come before My face with singing, enter My gates with thanksgiving and My courts with praise."*

Father wants His children close to Him, not beside Him, not in back of Him, not simply in front of Him, but *"in His face."* Get in the face of God. You will have His full attention, and He will have yours.

To be invited to get in the face of the Lord shows favor, partiality, respect, and acceptance. When the Lord says, *"Come before My presence,"* He is letting you know that He has accepted you. He is giving you an audience with the King of all the ages. He is not just allowing you to get near to Him; He is actually inviting you to approach Him. You are received by Him, *face to face.*

> *For God, who commanded the light to shine out of darkness, hath shined in our hearts, to give the light of the knowledge of the glory of God in the face of Jesus Christ.*   2 Corinthians 4:6 (KJV)

The face of God radiates His glory. It glows with His grace. It communicates to you His undying and never-ending love. Nothing could be more wonderful than to be in the face of God or, as the scriptures call it, *face to face.*

> *And Jacob called the name of the place Peniel: "For I*
> *have seen God face to face, and my life is preserved."*
>   Genesis 32:30

> *And the Lord spoke unto Moses face to face, as a*
> *man speaks to his friend.*   Exodus 33:11 (KJV)

Face to face is a term that speaks of intimacy with God. In modern terms, we might say that they were so close, they were *cheek to cheek.* Many of Moses' companions feared this intimacy with God.

> *"The Lord talked with you face to face on the moun-*
> *tain from the midst of the fire.*
> *"For you were afraid because of the fire, and you did*
> *not go up the mountain."*   Deuteronomy 5:4-5

Even today many Christians are afraid to get too close to God. They are accustomed to living their lives without God's presence. They are afraid to draw near to Him, some for fear of the unknown and others for fear that they will become too spiritual for those around them and lose their friends.

We seem to have our lives so well ordered these days. There is the secular, and there is the sacred. There is a time for the secular, and there is a time for the sacred. Although most of us believe that there is a time to be spiritual, we usually reserve that time for a church service. The rest of the time we live much as the rest of the world, doing what we want to do.

The Christian life, however, is a new life-style. It begins the day we are made a new creation in Christ, and it must not end until we are in the ultimate presence of God. God is calling us to be spiritual all the time, to live in His face, to walk in the Spirit every moment of every day.

If we live in the Spirit, let us also walk in the Spirit.
                                                    Galatians 5:25

This I say then, Walk in the Spirit, and you shall not fulfil the lust of the flesh.   Galatians 5:16 (KJV)

We are called to be spiritual, to walk in the Spirit, to live *face to face* with God. This is normal Christian living. Because there is so much carnality in the Church today, we consider someone who has a life-style of seeking God to be unusual. This is sad. Living close to God should be the norm of daily Christian life, not the rare exception. May the Lord bring us back to the place of desiring His presence and seeking His face.

His Manifest Presence at Creation

There are many examples of God manifesting or revealing His presence in unusual ways. These manifestations were very tangible and could be discerned by the natural senses. God revealed Himself in the creation.

In the beginning God created the heavens and the earth. Now the earth was formless and empty, darkness was over the surface of the deep, and the Spirit of God was hovering over the waters.
                                                    Genesis 1:1-2 (NIV)

In the beginning, there was an awareness of the presence of the Holy Spirit. He hovered over the waters. Although He, as the omnipotent God, was *in* the waters, *under* the waters and *beside* the waters, there was a definite concentration of His presence, a greater dimension of His presence, *over* the waters. His presence was manifested and moved *over* the waters more than it did *in* the waters, *under* the waters or *beside* the waters.

> *And God said, "Let there be light," and there*
> *was light.*   Genesis 1:3 (NIV)

In creation, God manifested His presence. He spoke and began to construct — from the nothing that existed before creation — everything that now exists. God manifested His presence through the creation of the animal, mineral, and vegetable kingdoms. He manifested His presence through the creation of a unique creature, whom he called "*man.*" Our very existence is testimony to the loving presence of God.

> *The Lord God formed the man from the dust of the*
> *ground and breathed into his nostrils the breath of life,*
> *and the man became a living being.*
>   Genesis 2:7 (NIV)

God manifest His presence by putting life into Adam and making him *a living being.* That life came from the power of His presence. He made a special place for Adam to live.

Now the Lord God had planted a garden in the east, in Eden, and there He put the man He had formed.
Genesis 2:8 (NIV)

God manifested His presence by preparing a garden for man. Eden was an emblem of His love, a result of His presence. As a hen patiently and carefully prepares a nest for its chicks, God formed a special place for His creation to dwell in goodness and safety. Then He manifested His presence by placing Adam into the garden He had so lovingly prepared.

God manifested His presence in making Adam a companion. In a remarkable exercise of His power, God proved His love for man in a very special way.

So the Lord God caused the man to fall into a deep sleep; and while he was sleeping, he took one of the man's ribs and closed up the place with flesh. Then the Lord God made a woman from the rib he had taken out of the man, and he brought her to the man.
Genesis 2:21-22 (NIV)

God's manifest presence produced a woman and placed her by Adam' side. There now existed a divinely matched couple. What a powerful demonstration of the loving presence of our heavenly Father!

Adam and Eve lived in an ideal setting. They had everything they needed. They were safe. They had nothing to worry about. Life, for them, was not a daily struggle for existence but a joyful walk with God and with each other. They were "set for life," an indication of God's special concern for them. God's presence and man's existence were inseparable.

His Manifest Presence in the Garden

Sin changed everything. After the man and the women realized that they had sinned, the thought of seeing God was no longer a pleasant one. They were afraid of His presence. They dreaded His coming. When He did come, they hid from Him.

> *Then the man and his wife heard the sound of the Lord God as He was walking in the garden in the cool of the day, and they hid from the Lord God among the trees of the garden. But the Lord God called to the man, "Where are you?" He answered, "I heard you in the garden, and I was afraid because I was naked; so I hid."*   Genesis 3:8-10 (NIV)

God and man had formed a custom of walking and talking together. Each looked forward to these moments of intimate communion. This was a very real experience. God made a sound as He walked in the garden, and Adam and Eve knew this sound. They had enjoyed the manifest presence of the Lord on many occasions.

Until now, the sound of the Lord had spoken to them of the power of their Creator, of Him who loved them and kept them, who taught them, who answered their every question and who could be relied upon totally. He was everything to them. But now, everything was changed. Sin destroyed man's joy in the presence of God.

When Adam and Eve heard the sound of God walking in the garden this time, they were not pleased. They were frightened. They knew they had let Him down.

Nevertheless, God spoke to Adam and Eve and asked them where they were. They were no longer *face to face* with Him, and that saddened Him. They were hiding from His presence in shame. Nothing could have affected Him more deeply.

In the aftermath of the fall, more damage was done to the relationship. The result of the fall was a curse upon the man, a curse upon the woman and a curse upon the serpent. The greatest part of the curse, for man, was his banishment from the garden. For he could no longer walk and talk with His Creator.

> *And the Lord God said, "The man has now become like one of us ... ." So the Lord God banished him from the Garden of Eden ... . He drove the man out.*
> Genesis 3:22-24 (NIV)

Although this part of the curse was directed to the man, it seems clear that the woman was also banished from the garden, as well as the serpent. From that day on, the serpent would crawl on his belly and eat the dust of the earth.

There are many lessons we can draw from these events, but the greatest must be that it is a bad omen for a man or woman when they are afraid of the presence of God and want to hide themselves. We were created for fellowship with God.

Even many religious people are guilty of hiding behind their liturgies and programs. They too are afraid of meeting with God personally. Religion is never a proper substitute for a personal relationship with the Father. His desire is for intimate communion.

The tragic thing is that God didn't go to the garden to condemn Adam and Eve. He went, as always, to have fellowship with them. Surely, if they had repented of their wrong and asked His forgiveness, it would have been readily granted. His mercy is great.

Don't hide yourself from God's presence for any reason. He wants you to get into His face. If there is sin in your heart, confess it to the Lord, turn from it, and then come into His presence with rejoicing.

His Manifest Presence to the Sons of Adam

In the course of time Cain brought some of the fruits of the soil as an offering to the Lord. ... The Lord looked with favor on Abel and his offering, but on Cain and his offering he did not look with favor.

Genesis 4:3-4 (NIV)

With time, men learned to offer an atonement for sin (an animal sacrifice) — in order to restore their broken relationship with God. Although the details are not given in the scriptural account, it is apparent that Cain and Abel regularly experienced some dimension of the manifest presence of God. They had developed a custom of approaching Him and communing with Him. On this occasion, they brought Him offerings.

This incident ended in a second tragedy for the first family on the earth because God was not pleased with the offering which Cain brought. Instead of repenting for having disobeyed God in the matter of sacrifices, Cain became angry and jealous of his brother and killed him — bringing a special curse upon his own life in the process.

> *"You will be a restless wanderer on the earth." Cain said to the Lord, "My punishment is more than I can bear. Today you are driving me from the land, and I will be hidden from your presence."*
>
> Genesis 4:12-14 (NIV)

Cain understood that he was being expelled from God's manifest presence.

> *So Cain went out from the Lord's presence .*
>
> Genesis 4:16 (NIV)

The descendants of Cain lived a life far from God and His favor. Typical of them was Lamech, the murderer.

What loneliness Cain must have borne! What deprivation! No wonder he said to God, *"My punishment is more than I can bear."* Would this banishment be man's permanent legacy? Or would God find a way for man to return to His loving presence?

His Manifest Presence at the Tower of Babel

About 2500 B.C., in the area known as Babylon, Adam's ambitious descendents decided to build a great city, which they called Babel. The work went so well that they became giddy with success and decided that they would build a tower so high it would *"reach to the heavens."* God was not pleased with their arrogance and felt that He must intervene in their affairs. The effects of what He did that day are still felt around the world, for He came down to *"confuse their language,"* and, thus, to cause them to scatter throughout the earth.

> *Then they said, "Come, let us build ourselves a city, with a tower that reaches to the heavens, so that we may make a name for ourselves and not be scattered over the face of the whole earth." But the Lord came down to see the city and the tower that the men were building. The Lord said, ... "Come, let us go down and confuse their language so they will not understand each other."*   Genesis 11:4-7 (NIV)

The Lord *"came down."* He was there all the time by His omnipresence, but He decided to manifest His presence or to *"come down."* This is what has come to be known as a *theophany*, an appearance by God. His appearance here was not a happy occasion. He *"came down"* to investigate the pride and the wicked intentions of the people of Babel and to execute judgement upon them. God's presence to judge and to mete out punishment is very real.

The *"us"* of *"let Us go down,"* is the same term that was used for the Trinity in the creation account. There is no mistaking this divine intervention into the affairs of man.

This was the beginning of not only diverse languages but also of diverse peoples. For the first time, mankind was divided into clans, nations, and even various ethnic groups — all this a result of the power of God's manifest presence.

> *The Lord confused the language of the whole world. From there the Lord scattered them over the face of the whole earth.*   Genesis 11:9 (NIV)

His Manifest Presence in the Burning Bush

I consider the burning bush to be one the most unusual expression of God's manifest presence in Bible history. God showed Himself to Moses in a bush that burned with fire and yet was not devoured.

> *And the angel of the Lord appeared unto him in a flame of fire out of the midst of a bush: and he looked, and, behold, the bush burned with fire, and the bush was not consumed. And Moses said, I will now turn aside and see this great sight, why the bush is not burnt. And when the Lord saw that he turned aside to see, God called unto him out of the midst of the bush, and said, Moses, Moses. And he said, Here am I.*   Exodus 3:2-4 (KJV)

How interesting! *The angel of the Lord* was in the fire, and God called to Moses out of the middle of the burning bush. Later, we will discuss the significance of this phenomena. God revealed His presence to Moses through the miracle of the burning bush.

> *And He said, Draw not nigh hither; put off thy shoes*
> *from off thy feet, for the place whereon thou standest is*
> *holy ground. Moreover He said I am God of thy father,*
> *the God Abraham, the God of Isaac, and the God of*
> *Jacob. And Moses hid his face; for he was afraid to look*
> *upon God.*   Exodus 3:5-6 (KJV)

Moses knew that he was in God's holy presence. With an overwhelming sense of God's nearness, he hid his face and bowed toward the bush which burned with the fire of God's manifest presence. Sometimes I feel the same way when I have an encounter with the King of all kings and Lord of all Lords.

His Manifest Presence in Egypt

When God's presence appeared to administer discipline, it was not out of a desire for vengeance or a desire to strike back, but out of love and a desire to lead His people to repentance. Sometimes this intervention took the form of plagues.

The presence of Moses before Pharaoh would bring plagues. In this case, Moses was blamed; but the plagues were the direct result of the presence of an angry God (Who would judge Pharaoh for his stubbornness and his refusal to recognize and worship the true God). The plagues demonstrated God's ability to deliver His people and they demonstrated His presence with them.

Rods become snakes; water become blood; frogs, gnats, and flies appeared; animals died, people got boils; hail and locusts destroyed vegetation; and darkness covered the land (Exodus 7, 8 and 9).

Pharaoh's magicians responded with artificial manifestations of power, human trickery, devised to counterfeit the true miracles of God, and with the manifestation of demon power.

When Pharaoh refused to humble himself before his Creator, God manifested His presence in one last blow:

> *"This is what the Lord says: 'About midnight I will go throughout Egypt. Every firstborn son in Egypt will die, from the firstborn son of Pharaoh, who sits on the throne, to the firstborn son of the slave girl, who is at her hand mill, and all the firstborn of the cattle as well."* Exodus 11:4-5 (NIV)

"I will go throughout Egypt." Under other circumstances those words might bring joy. In this case, however, God's presence would bring death and agony of soul to every unprotected home. The manifest presence of the living God was so awesome that both men and animals died as He passed. The unrepentant Rameses and his subjects learned a hard lesson that night, while the Hebrews, who had obediently applied the blood of a one-year-old, male lamb or goat to the sideposts and lintels of the doors of their homes, were protected.

> *"On that same night I will pass through Egypt and strike down every firstborn—both men and animals—and I will bring judgement on all the gods of Egypt. I am the Lord. The blood will be a sign for you*

> *on the houses where you are; and when I see the blood,*
> *I will pass over you."*   Exodus 12:12-13 (NIV)

As the awesome presence of God passed through the homes in Egypt, it left its mark on each one: on those which were not covered by the blood, death and destruction, on those that were, the joy of life and liberty. Before long, a great cry was heard in the land. The unbelieving were mourning their loss, and the believing were rejoicing over their deliverance.

> *There was loud wailing in Egypt, for there was not a*
> *house without someone dead.*
>   Exodus 12:30 (NIV)

Having seen the manifestation of His power, Rameses let God's people go.

His Manifest Presence in the Cloud and the Fire

> *By day the Lord went ahead of them in a pillar of cloud*
> *to guide them on their way and by night in a pillar of*
> *fire to give them light, so that they could travel by day*
> *or night. Neither the pillar of cloud by day nor the*
> *pillar of fire by night left its place in front of the people.*
>   Exodus 13:21-22 (NIV)

As the children of Israel left Egypt and traveled toward the Promised Land, God's presence with them was made visible. It could be seen by everyone with the natural eye. During the daytime, His presence was seen as a column of cloud and, at night, it appeared as a column of fire. None could doubt His presence! It was manifest to all.

This cloud of God's presence protected the children of Israel.

> *Then the angel of God, who had been traveling in front of Israel's army, withdrew and went behind them. The pillar of cloud also moved from in front and stood behind them, coming between the armies of Egypt and Israel. Throughout the night the cloud brought darkness to the one side and light to the other side; so neither went near the other all night long.*
>
> Exodus 14:19-20 (NIV)

God Himself stood between the armies of Pharaoh and the escaping people of Israel. The phrase *"Angel of God"* is believed by most Bible scholars to be an expression of Deity. It is not believed, however, to be Jehovah Himself, but perhaps a manifestation of the Son of God, the pre-incarnate Logos, in Old Testament times. He was with the Father in creation, and here perhaps we see Him again, long before He came to earth in the form of a man.

Whatever the case, it is a clear manifestation of the presence of the Lord. He was there to protect Israel.

> *During the last watch of the night the Lord looked down from the pillar of fire and cloud at the Egyptian army and threw it into confusion. He made the wheels of their chariots come off so that they had difficulty driving. And the Egyptians said, "Let's get away*

*from the Israelites! The Lord is fighting for them
against Egypt!"*   Exodus 14:24-25 (NIV)

Even the heathen Egyptians had to acknowledge that
what they were witnessing was the work of the presence
of the Lord of Israel. Neither side doubted His presence.

This fire of God's presence fell upon those Israelites
who rebelled against Moses' leadership in the desert.

*Fire came out from the Lord and consumed the 250
men who were offering the incense.*
                                Numbers 16:35 (NIV)

What a powerful demonstration of God's presence! Fire
came from His presence and struck two hundred and fifty
men at the same time. The next day, a worse thing happened, causing the death of nearly fifteen thousand more
Israelites; and if Aaron had not intervened, even more
would have died.

*The next day the whole Israelite community grumbled
against Moses and Aaron. "You have killed the Lord's
people," they said. But when the assembly gathered in
opposition to Moses and Aaron and turned toward
the Tent of Meeting, suddenly the cloud covered it
and the glory of the Lord appeared. Then Moses and
Aaron went to the front of the Tent of Meeting, and
the Lord said to Moses, "Get away from this assembly
so I can put an end to them at once." And they fell face
down. ... The plague had already started among the*

> *people, but Aaron offered the incense and made atone-*
> *ment for them. He stood between the living and the*
> *dead, and the plague stopped. But 14,700 people died*
> *from the plague.* Numbers 16:41-49 (NIV)

Everyone knew that God was present.

When the cloud moved, the children of Israel were to pack up and move. When the cloud stayed, they were to halt their march and make camp. When the cloud descended, it was a signal to Moses that God wanted to meet with Him in a special way. He had something special to say to His servant.

When we sense that God desires to call us aside, we should drop everything we are doing and rush to His presence. He has some wonderful things to say to us. Perhaps we don't see a visible cloud of His presence, but He will make known to us His desire to commune.

Aside from being for protection and guidance, the cloud served many other purposes. It protected Israel from the hot sun of the desert. Since it turned into a pillar of fire at night, the cloud became light for them in the midst of darkness.

What a wonderful sanctuary! What tremendous benefits we reap from the presence of God in our lives! Nothing can compare to it. No insurance policy can replace it. Don't be without God's presence — even for a single moment.

Because they faithfully followed the presence of God in the cloud and in the fire, the Hebrew children eventually arrived safely at the crossing of the Jordan River.

> *When the cloud was taken up from above the taber-*
> *nacle, the children of Israel went onward in all their*
> *journeys. But if the cloud was not taken up, then they*
> *did not journey till the day that it was taken up. For*
> *the cloud of the Lord was above the tabernacle by day,*
> *and fire was over it by night, in the sight of all the*
> *house of Israel, throughout all their journeys.*
>
> Exodus 40:36-38

His Manifest Presence on Sinai

When Israel came to the desert of Sinai, Moses went up into a mountain to meet with God. This mountain is referred to in the Bible as *Mount Sinai*. The exact location of the mountain in question is not known; what is known is that God met Moses there.

> *Then Moses went up to God, and the Lord called to*
> *him from the mountain.*   Exodus 19:3 (NIV)

As Moses went up the mountain, the presence of God became visible or manifest. He felt the nearness of God and heard the voice of His Lord.

On other days, the presence of God on the mountain was manifested in strange ways that caused the people to tremble with fear. Thunder and lightning, the sound of a trumpet and a *"thick cloud over the mountain"* were all evidence that God was near. When Moses led the people out of the camp toward the mountain to meet with God, smoke ascended from the mountain as from a great furnace. The sound of the trumpet grew louder, and the ground around the whole area shook.

> *On the morning of the third day there was thunder
> and lightning, with a thick cloud over the mountain,
> and a very loud trumpet blast. Everyone in the camp
> trembled. Then Moses led the people out of the camp to
> meet with God, and they stood at the foot of the moun-
> tain. Mount Sinai was covered with smoke, because
> the Lord descended on it in fire. The smoke billowed up
> from it like smoke from a furnace, the whole mountain
> trembled violently, and the sound of the trumpet grew
> louder and louder. Then Moses spoke and the voice of
> God answered him.* Exodus 19:16-19 (NIV)

That demonstration of the power of God's presence was
never forgotten in Israel. David remembered it as he sang
before the Lord on Mount Zion many years later:

> *O God when You went out before Your people,*
> *When You marched through the wilderness,*
> *The earth shook;*
> *The heavens also dropped rain at the presence of God;*
> *Sinai itself was moved at the presence of God, the God*
> *of Israel.* Psalms 68:7-8

Some of our modern people would not have been comfortable at Mount Sinai. They are uncomfortable when
God reveals His presence by healing the sick and raising
the dead, by people being slain in the power of God or
through loud praise. Yet these are all evidences of God's
presence with His people.

Many people don't like loud demonstration. They are
more comfortable with a god who is invisible and who

never reveals his presence. Surprisingly, some of Moses'
companions felt the same way.

> *When the people saw the thunder and lightning and*
> *heard the trumpet and saw the mountain in smoke,*
> *they trembled with fear. They stayed at a distance and*
> *said to Moses, "Speak to us yourself and we will lis-*
> *ten. But do not have God speak to us or we will die."*
> Exodus 20:18-19 (NIV)

This was too much for some. God was *too present* for
their liking. Moses was a friend of God, but most of the
Israelites did not share such a strong relationship with
their God. They were satisfied to hear from Him through
Moses. This was too much for them and, sadly, was the
cause of God's withdrawal to a safe distance.

What frightened some of them was that Moses and the
elders of Israel were not only blessed to see the presence of
God on this mountain; they were permitted to actually see
God.

> *Moses and Aaron ... and the seventy elder of Israel*
> *went up and saw the God of Israel. Under his feet was*
> *something like a pavement made of sapphire, clear as*
> *the sky itself. But God did not raise his hand against*
> *these leaders of the Israelites; they saw God and they*
> *ate and drank.*   Exodus 24:9-11 (NIV)

Many people have seen the manifest presence of God;
but these men actually saw God. What an experience!

> *When Moses went up on the mountain, the cloud*
> *covered it, and the glory of the Lord settled on Mount*
> *Sinai. For six days the cloud covered the mountain,*
> *and on the seventh day the Lord called to Moses from*
> *within the cloud. To the Israelites the glory of the Lord*
> *looked like a consuming fire on top of the mountain.*
> *Then Moses entered the cloud as he went on up the*
> *mountain.* Exodus 24:15-18 (NIV)

Because most men were not comfortable with the manifestation of God's presence in their daily lives, God was forced to withdraw Himself to what they considered to be a safer distance. While Moses visited with God on Mount Sinai, God gave him detailed instructions for the design and construction of a place of worship. It was to be called a *tabernacle* or *tent of meeting* and would be a place where men could encounter the manifest presence of God.

Since the people of Israel, in general, wanted no part of God's manifest presence in their daily lives, He would contain it in a sanctuary and allow a privileged few, of His choice, to come before Him there.

His Manifest Presence in the Tabernacle

The tabernacle that God described to Moses was to be a place filled with God's holy presence. When we study the tabernacle, we are often caught up with the elaborate detail of its design (and that of its furnishings and of the priests who would administer the holy place and of their clothing), and forget its purpose.

The elaborate preparations for the tabernacle are indeed fascinating. They suggest to us that no detail of man's worship of God is too small for His concern. He is interested in men coming into His presence and wants to make His presence more available to His people. This is, clearly, the most important thing in our lives.

Every effort was made to make the tabernacle, its furnishings and its administrators pure. This is an indication of how strongly God feels about the purity of His people.

The tabernacle was built by Moses and Israel according to God's specific instructions (Exodus 40). When it was finished, the manifest presence of God came to dwell there.

> *Then the cloud covered the Tent of Meeting, and the glory of the Lord filled the tabernacle. Moses could not enter the Tent of Meeting because the cloud had settled upon it, and the glory of the Lord filled the tabernacle.*   Exodus 40:34-35 (NIV)

The presence of God was called here *the glory of the Lord*. Later, we will discuss the importance of this term.

His Manifest Presence Above the Ark

Another manifestation of God's presence in Old Testament history concerns the Ark of the Covenant, also known as "the Ark of the Testimony" and "the Ark of the Lord." The Ark was a wooden box, but it was much more than a box. The beaten gold that covered it inside and out was not what made it so special. The Ark was a symbol of God's presence with His people.

To the Israelites, the Ark was most sacred and was the center of attention in the camp. They considered it to be the place where God dwelt, as well as His throne. It was at the Ark of the Covenant that Moses and other ancients met God *face to face*. When Moses entered the Tent of Meeting to speak with the Lord, he heard God's voice speaking to him from between the two cherubim above the atonement cover on the Ark of the Testimony.

> *So the people sent to Shiloh, that they might bring from thence the ark of the covenant of the Lord of hosts, who dwells between the cherubim.*
>
> 1 Samuel 4:4

Because the Ark was so important, the tabernacle was designed with the ark as its centerpiece. Everything else revolved around it. Three matching entrances led to it. Without the Ark and the presence of God that it represented, the tabernacle had no purpose. Those who entered the tabernacle did so because the presence of God dwelt in the Ark of the Covenant.

Once the tabernacle was built, the Ark was secured behind the veil of the Holy of Holies, a room reserved for Moses (when the Lord called him to enter) and the high priest (on the day of atonement).

Throughout Israel's generations, going through the veil was viewed as tantamount to suicide. Even the high priest entered the room with extreme caution. If, for some reason, he was unclean in God's sight when he entered the Holy of Holies, he would be immediately struck dead. Historians have recorded that the high priests tied a long rope onto one ankle and left one end of the rope outside the Most Holy Place so that the body of any priest slain by the presence of God could be recovered.

This has been a reminder to all generations that although God is willing to manifest His presence to His people, He does so on His own terms, not according to the whims of carnal man.

Traditionally, Israel sought guidance and direction from God at the Ark.

> *Then all the children of Israel ... came unto the house of God, and wept, and sat there before the Lord, and fasted that day until even ... and enquired of the Lord, (for the ark of the covenant of God was there in those days) ... . And the Lord said, Go up.*
>
> Judges 20:26-28 (KJV)

God's presence gives us direction for our lives. He is our inspiration. Are we listening to what He is trying to say to us? Or are we doing all the talking and not giving Him a chance to speak? Sometimes we need to be still and listen, even in prayer. It is a two-way conversation.

The Israelites never worshiped the Ark. The Ark was not God. God used the Ark to manifest His presence. He dwelt between the cherubim *on* the ark of the covenant.

Because of all that God's presence did for them, the Israelites held the Ark as their most prized possession. The presence of the Ark was a reason for great rejoicing and, when it was missing, a cause for great concern. We are able to witness that fact in the account of its return, after having been captured in battle.

> *And when the ark of the covenant of the Lord came
> into the camp, all Israel shouted with a great shout, so
> that the earth rang again.*   1 Samuel 4:5 (KJV)

> *So David, and the elders of Israel, and the captains
> over thousands, went to bring up the ark of the cov-
> enant of the Lord out of the house of Obed-edom
> with joy.*   1 Chronicles 15:25 (KJV)

The manifestation of God's presence in the midst of
those who love Him will always bring joy. The people of
God have a right to shout. We have cause for celebration.

When we have sin in our lives, the presence of God
causes fear. Sin separates us from God. Deal with the sin
in your life so that you can enjoy God's presence as He
intended.

Some Christians get upset when they see others rejoicing. They equate loudness and jubilance with sinful
behavior. But that is not always true. God created joyful-
ness and celebration. Satan often tries to copy what God
has ordained for His people. It is normal to be jubilant
when God reveals Himself to you.

> *Thus all Israel brought up the ark of the covenant of
> the Lord with shouting, and with sound of the cornet,
> and with trumpets, and with cymbals, making a noise
> with psalteries and harps.*
>   1 Chronicles 15:28 (KJV)

Dancing is another natural expression of joy in the presence of God that makes many people self-conscious and

uneasy — perhaps because of the connection they make to worldly dancing. They can't imagine that such behavior has a place in the church. But God intended dancing as a form of pure praise to Him.

Others are uncomfortable with dancing in worship because *they* are the center of worship. If *He* is the center of worship, you forget everything else and everybody else and worship spontaneously, regardless of what it might look like to others.

Let Christ be the focal point of your worship, not each other. When you become God-conscious, you will no longer worry about what other people think about you or how you look in their eyes.

When David danced before the Lord, his wife, Michal, was offended. She was the daughter of Saul, and she considered David's actions to be undignified for a king.

> *And it came to pass, as the ark of the covenant of the Lord came to the city of David, that Michal the daughter of Saul looking out at a window saw king David dancing and playing: and she despised him in her heart.*   1 Chronicles 15:29 (KJV)

David, however, could did not let Michal's lack of understanding dampen his fervor to God. He knew that God deserves the very best of our praise. She was punished with barrenness because of her attitude toward David's whole-hearted worship.

Praise became the normal order of the day before the Ark of the Lord.

Benaiah also and Jahaziel the priests with trumpets continually before the ark of the covenant of God.
                    1 Chronicles 16:6 (KJV)

So he left there before the ark of the covenant of the Lord Asaph and his brethren, to minister before the ark continually, as every day's work required:
And with them Heman and Jeduthun with trumpets and cymbals for those that should make a sound, and with musical instruments of God.
                    1 Chronicles 16:37 & 42 (KJV)

The Ark was Israel's secret weapon in combat. The armies of Israel would take this box, on which God's presence was, to war with them. The Ark could not be carried forth into battle against the enemy by just anyone. It could only be handled by the descendents of Levi.

At that time the Lord separated the tribe of Levi, to bear the ark of the covenant of the Lord, to stand before the Lord to minister unto him, and to bless in his name, unto this day.   Deuteronomy 10:8 (KJV)

Joshua had the Ark carried into battle when he fought against Jericho. The children of Israel had no military power apart from the Lord. They had no trained armies, no experienced generals. For four hundred years they had served as slaves, making bricks and building cities. What did they know of battle?

Along the way from Egypt, they had picked up assorted weapons from the tribes they battled; but they could not have made war successfully against organized military powers — except that they had a secret weapon: the presence of their God.

> *Joshua rose early in the morning, and the priests took up the ark of the Lord. And seven priests bearing seven trumpets of rams' horns before the ark of the Lord went on continually, and blew with the trumpets: and the armed men went before them; but the rereward came after the ark of the Lord, the priests going on, and blowing with the trumpets.*
>
> Joshua 6:12-13 (KJV)

It wasn't long before the enemies of Israel learned the secret: With the Ark, Israel was invincible in battle. If the Ark could be captured, Israel could be defeated. The tactic of every enemy became, therefore, to isolate and capture the Ark.

> *And when the Philistines heard the noise of the shout, they said, What meaneth the noise of this great shout in the camp of the Hebrews? And they understood that the ark of the Lord was come into the camp.*
>
> 1 Samuel 4:6 (KJV)

When we celebrate the presence of the Lord in our midst, that lets every enemy know that God is with us and that we cannot be defeated. Every principality and power of spiritual wickedness in heavenly places is afraid of the mighty presence of God and is powerless to attack us — when He is near. Every enemy bows in His presence.

> *When they ... arose early on the morrow, behold,*
> *Dagon was fallen upon his face to the earth before the*
> *ark of the Lord. And they took Dagon, and set him in*
> *his place again. And when they arose early on the*
> *morrow morning, behold, Dagon was fallen upon his*
> *face to the ground before the ark of the Lord; and the*
> *head of Dagon and both the palms of his hands were*
> *cut off upon the threshold; only the stump of Dagon*
> *was left to him.*   1 Samuel 5:3-4 (KJV)

At the presence of the Lord of Hosts other gods fall. The manifestation of God's presence has a chilling effect on our common enemies.

When Solomon became king, he continued to honor the Ark and the God of the Ark.

> *And Solomon ... came to Jerusalem, and stood before*
> *the ark of the covenant of the Lord, and offered up*
> *burnt offerings, and offered peace offerings, and made*
> *a feast to all his servants.*   1 Kings 3:15 (KJV)

Solomon knew that when he stood before the Ark, he was standing before God. He was in the revealed presence of the Almighty.

Since 586 B.C., when the armies of the famous Nebuchadnezzar sacked the city of Jerusalem and carried away or destroyed the Ark, Jews have felt their great loss. Some believe that Israel can never be great again until the Ark is found and restored to its place in everyday Jewish life. Much effort is given to its recovery.

As Christians, however, we know that when Jesus rose from the dead, the veil of the Temple was torn in two by an invisible hand, signifying that all men could now enter into the Holy of Holies and experience God's presence for themselves, without fear. Was this not God's will from the beginning?

Today, you are the ark of the covenant. God's glory rests upon you. You are the carrier of His presence. Wherever you go, the manifest presence of God can and should go too. God is calling you to be a testimony to the nations that God lives among those who love Him.

His Manifest Presence as *the Glory of the Lord*

The glory of the Lord is a term very few people understand or can accurately define. Yet it is something we read about often in scripture and mention often in our preaching of the Word of God. What is *the glory of the Lord*?

The glory of the Lord is *an exhibition of the excellence of God, the display of His divine attributes and perfection.* This is a reference to the manifestation of God's presence. Forty-five times the word translated *glory* is *kabod*. It signifies a visible manifestation of God. Most of those forty-five uses of this word are related to the tabernacle. In the tabernacle, man came in contact with *the glory of the Lord*. Other uses of the word were related to the temple that Ezekiel saw in vision. Often the word is associated with God's holiness.

God wants to reveal His glory, His splendor. He wants to disclose Himself to man. He wants to dwell among us and fellowship with us. He wants to share with us His holiness.

Once, when I was in a church service somewhere in the south, a woman came up to me after the meeting and said that she had seen a cloud fill the church building as we were singing and praising the Lord. Why not? God wants to show us His glory.

When the tabernacle was finished and the priests were ready to begin their ministry there, Moses called everyone to gather before the tent for the dedication.

> *And Moses said, "This is the thing which the Lord commanded you to do, and **the glory of the Lord** will appear to you."* Leviticus 9:6

They were expecting to see the presence of the Lord in a physical sense, and they were not disappointed. Once the prescribed offerings had been placed on the altar — the calf, the goat, the grain, the bull, and the ram — something unusual happened.

> *And Moses and Aaron went into the tabernacle of the congregation, and came out, and blessed the people: and **the glory of the Lord** appeared unto all the people. And there came a fire out from before the Lord, and consumed upon the altar the burnt offering and the fat: which, when all the people saw, they shouted, and fell on their faces.* Leviticus 9:23-24 (KJV)

The glory of the Lord is a visible manifestation of God. It is something that can be seen. It is an exhibition or display of the splendor of the Lord.

It is often seen as light. Light is a part of the nature of God, and when we enter His presence, the light of His nearness may fill the place where we are gathered. Others may see it in a different way — as fire perhaps.

The glory of the Lord appeared in the tabernacle. It was apparent for all to see.

> And **the glory of the Lord** *appeared in the tabernacle of the congregation before all the children of Israel*
>   Numbers 14:10 (KJV)

Everyone could see this unusual manifestation of God's presence (Numbers 16:19). It was *"before all the children of Israel."*

> *And it came to pass, when the congregation was gathered against Moses and against Aaron, that they looked toward the tabernacle of the congregation: and, behold, the cloud covered it, and* **the glory of the Lord** *appeared.*   Numbers 16:42 (KJV)

Someday, the Bible declares, the whole world will be filled with this manifestation of God's presence, His glory.

> *But as truly as I live, all the earth shall be filled with* **the glory of the Lord***.*   Numbers 14:21 (KJV)

Some have suggested that only the reputation of God's greatness will fill the earth, but why should we limit God? The whole earth will be literally filled with the reality of His presence. His desire has always been that all men of all nations would recognize Him and worship Him for who He is. I believe this promise literally and hold to it in great expectation.

> *The glory of the Lord shall be revealed, and all flesh shall see it together: For the mouth of the Lord hath spoken it.*   Isaiah 40:5 (KJV)

What an outstanding prophecy! All flesh will see the manifest glory of God.

There will come a time when all living persons will know about the glory of the Lord. Everyone will be aware of God's manifest presence in the world. His presence will inundate every continent, every country on every continent, every city in every country on every continent, and every community within every city in every country on every continent. If people have not experienced the presence of God for themselves, they will certainly hear about it from others.

> *For the earth will be filled with the knowledge of **the glory of the Lord**, as the waters cover the sea.*
> Habakkuk 2:14 (NIV)

In several recorded instances in scripture, this *glory of the Lord* was so powerfully evidenced that some people could not stand up. They fell down in the awesome presence of God.

> *And it came to pass, when the priests came out of the holy place, that the cloud filled the house of the Lord, so that the priests could not continue ministering*

> *because of the cloud; for **the glory of the Lord** filled*
> *the house of the Lord.*   1 Kings 8:10-11

People suddenly falling down while they are being prayed for is not uncommon these days in many church circles. It is possible that some fall because they have been pushed. Others may fall purposely, thinking that their friends will believe that God has really met them. But still others fall down without any apparent provocation or deliberation. This is often due to the power of the presence of God being manifested.

Some call this being "slain in the Spirit." The inference is that the Spirit of God has knocked them down. The presence of the Divine moving on the flesh of humans causes them to fall. Some people who fall in this way are unaware of what is happening around them for a period of time, sometimes for only a few minutes, but sometimes for much longer. They lay that way for a time (while God talks to them and works on them); then they return to consciousness.

Many of those who have this experience later describe in detail something they saw or heard during the time they were "slain." Some of them experience healing. Many of them have encountered *the glory of the Lord*. This can also happen in periods of deep worship.

> *Indeed it came to pass, when the trumpeters and sing-*
> *ers were as one, to make one sound to be heard in*
> *praising and thanking the Lord, and when they lifted*
> *up their voice with the trumpets and cymbals and*
> *instruments of music, and praised the Lord, saying:*

"For He is good,
For His mercy endures forever,"

that the house, the house of the Lord, was filled with a
cloud, so that the priests could not continue minis-
*tering because of the cloud; for **the glory of the Lord***
filled the house of God.   2 Chronicles 5:13-14

The place where God manifested His glory came to be
known as *the house of the Lord* or *the Lord's house* . Everyone
recognized that His presence was in that place.

And the priests could not enter into the house of the
*Lord, because **the glory of the Lord** had filled the*
Lord's house. And when all the children of Israel saw
*how the fire came down, and **the glory of the Lord***
upon the house, they bowed themselves with their
faces to the ground upon the pavement, and wor-
shipped, and praised the Lord, saying, For he is good;
for his mercy endureth for ever.
                                2 Chronicles 7:2-3 (KJV)

The glory of the Lord was not reserved for the priests. We
can all experience it.

*Arise, shine; for thy light is come, and **the glory of***
***the Lord** is risen upon thee.*   Isaiah 60:1 (KJV)

God wants to share His glory with you. He wants you to
come to the brightness of your rising. Then He wants His

presence in you to be a witness to those who do not know Him as their Lord and Savior.

Ezekiel saw *the glory of the Lord.*

> *Then the spirit took me up, and I heard behind me a voice of a great rushing, saying, Blessed be **the glory of the Lord** from his place.*   Ezekiel 3:12 (KJV)

> *Then I arose, and went forth into the plain: and, behold, **the glory of the Lord** stood there, as the glory which I saw by the river of Chebar: and I fell on my face.*   Ezekiel 3:23 (KJV)

> *Then **the glory of the Lord** went up from the cherub, and stood over the threshold of the house; and the house was filled with the cloud, and the court was full of the brightness of **the Lord's glory.***
> Ezekiel 10:4 (KJV)

> *And **the glory of the Lord** went up from the midst of the city, and stood upon the mountain which is on the east side of the city.*   Ezekiel 11:23 (KJV)

> *Then brought he me the way of the north gate before the house: and I looked, and, behold, **the glory of the Lord** filled the house of the Lord: and I fell upon my face.*   Ezekiel 44:4 (KJV)

When Jesus was born, some shepherds in Bethlehem saw *the glory of the Lord.* As they were watching their sheep that fateful night, they had a heavenly visitor. The Scriptures declare:

And, lo, the angel of the Lord came upon them, and
the glory of the Lord *shone round about them: and*
they were sore afraid. Luke 2:9 (KJV)

Two things are notable in this passage. The *angel of the
Lord* and *the glory of the Lord*. The two go together, as we
shall see. In this case, the glory of God was so overwhelming that these brave men, accustomed to the night, being
frequent companions of the stars, were now terrified by
what they saw, and it soon got worse.

*And suddenly there was with the angel a multitude of
the heavenly host praising God, and saying, Glory to
God in the highest, and on earth peace, good will
toward men.* Luke 2:13-14 (KJV)

First they saw *the angel of the Lord* and *the glory of the Lord*,
and now they saw a multitude of heavenly knights
coming out of the sky with a loud noise.

Some scholars say that this was a celestial army of light-
bearers marching from the sky lauding and boasting of
God in a set discourse, a heavenly army of luminaries
marching and praising God with a piece of music that was
previously prepared.

What an sight! No wonder the shepherds were
impressed!

Several times, while I have been leading people in worship, I have had visions of angelic activity in the
atmosphere. When I opened my eyes, I couldn't see angels, but I was very much aware that they were present,

moving about above our heads and singing in loud voices.

This usually happened, not when we were singing songs that we knew, but when we were singing spontaneously in praise to God from our hearts. When we sing something that we know, we are thinking too much about the words and the music and not enough about HIM. When we are not required to concentrate on a lyric and a melody, it is easier for us to enter another level of worship and see into another dimension.

According to the Bible, angels have musical ability and often sing adorations to the Lamb Who sits on the throne. The Bible also teaches that angels are very present with us. When we worship God, angels must get very excited, for that is what they enjoy most. They are creatures of worship and creatures of God's manifest presence.

The glory of the Lord was not just for the Old Testament.

> *But we all, with open face beholding as in a glass **the glory of the Lord**, are changed into the same image from glory to glory, even as by the Spirit of the Lord.*
> 2 Corinthians 3:18 (KJV)

We can *"all"* behold *the glory of the Lord*. Although the great majority of Christians have not experienced it, that doesn't change the promise. We can *"all"* behold His glory *"with open face"* or *with unrestricted vision*.

We need to take advantage of this promise; for, as we behold His glory, we are changed. A metamorphosis takes place in which we become like what we are beholding. We become like *the glory of the Lord*. And the more time we spend in the presence of God, the more we become like Him. We are *"changed into the same image."* We develop *"from glory to glory."* This miraculous metamorphosis can take place in the Spirit and in the presence of the Creator.

His Manifest Presence as the Angel of the Lord

The term *the angel of the Lord* is a theophany, an appearance by God in human form. Most Bible scholars believe that the angel of the Lord was none other than Jesus Christ, manifesting Himself in a tangible form.

> ***The angel of the Lord*** *found Hagar near a spring in the desert. ... And he said, "Hagar, servant of Sarai, where have you come from, and where are you going?"*
> *"I'm running away from my mistress Sarai," she answered. Then the angel of the Lord told her, "Go back to your mistress and submit to her." The angel added, "I will so increase your descendants that they will be too numerous to count."* Genesis 16:7-10 (NIV)

The angel of the Lord is the presence of the Lord or, at least, an expression of the presence of God. God saw Hagar in the desert and spoke with her there.

> ***The angel of the Lord*** *also said to her:*
> *"You are now with child and you will have a son.*
> *You shall name him Ishmael.*
> *He will live in hostility toward all his brothers."*
> Genesis 16:11-12 (NIV)

Who can deny the prophetic impact of these words. Until now the descendants of Ishmael live in hostility toward all their brothers, creating one of the most serious threats to peace in the world and causing all eyes to be on the Middle East. God said it would be so.

> *She gave this name to the Lord who spoke to her: "You are the God who sees me," for she said, "I have now seen the One who sees me."*   Genesis 16:13 (NIV)

Hagar realized that the person speaking to her was not just a man. She called Him *"Lord"* and even *"God."* Hagar was not alone. She was in the presence, *in the face,* of the Almighty. He knew who she was, understood her dilemma, and resolved her problem.

The angel of the Lord appeared to Abraham on Mt. Moriah.

> *When they reached the place God had told him about, Abraham built an altar there and arranged the wood on it. He bound his son Isaac and laid him on the altar, on top of the wood. Then he reached out his hand and took the knife to slay his son. But **the angel of the Lord** called out to him from heaven, "Abraham! Abraham!"*
>
> *"Here I am," he replied.*
>
> *"Do not lay a hand on the boy," he said. "Do not do anything to him. Now I know that you fear God, because you have not withheld from me your son, your only son."*   Genesis 22:9-12 (NIV)

We know that this "angel" is God because He said to Abraham, *"You have not withheld from ME your son."* Abraham knew that He was in the very presence of God. The angel spoke a second time.

> *The angel of the Lord called to Abraham from heaven a second time and said. "I swear by myself, declares the Lord, that because you have done this and have not withheld your son, your only son, I will surely bless you and make your descendants as numerous as the stars in the sky."*
>
> Genesis 22:15-17 (NIV)

"I swear by Myself, declares the Lord." If an angel had been speaking on the Lord's behalf, he would have spoken in the third person about God. He didn't. He spoke in the first person. This "angel" was God.

Samson's mother experienced the presence of God. He showed Himself to her as *the angel of the Lord.*

> *A certain man of Zorah, named Manoah, ... had a wife who was sterile and remained childless. The angel of the Lord appeared to her and said, "You are sterile and childless, but you are going to conceive and have a son.*
>
> *Then the woman went to her husband and told him, "A man of God came to me. He looked like an angel of God, very awesome. I didn't ask him where he came from, and he didn't tell me his name."*
>
> Judges 13:2-3 & 6 (NIV)

In describing what she had seen and heard to her husband, Samson's mother called the angel *"a man of God."* *"He looked,"* she said, *"like an angel of God."* How interesting! *"Very awesome!"* were her words.

Later Manoah saw the angel for himself.

> **The angel of the Lord** *came again to the woman while she was out in the field.*
>
> *Manoah said to* **the angel of the Lord***, "We would like you to stay until we prepare a young goat for you."*
>
> **The angel of the Lord** *replied, "Even though you detain me, I will not eat any of your food. But if you prepare a burnt offering, offer it to the Lord."*
>
> *Then Manoah inquired of the angel of the Lord, "What is your name, so that we may honor you when your word comes true?"*
>
> *He replied, "Why do you ask my name? It is beyond understanding." Then Manoah took a young goat, together with the grain offering, and sacrificed it on a rock to the Lord. And the Lord did an amazing thing while Manoah and his wife watched: As the flame blazed up from the altar toward heaven,* **the angel of the Lord** *ascended in the flame. Seeing this, Manoah and his wife fell with their faces to the ground. When* **the angel of the Lord** *did not show himself again to Manoah and his wife, Manoah realized that it was the angel of the Lord.*
>
> *"We are doomed to die!" he said to his wife. "We have seen God!"*   Judges 13:9 & 15-22 (NIV)

At first, Manoah did not realize that he was talking to God. He asked the angel's name, perhaps thinking that it was a man. When the angel *"ascended in the flame,"* all doubt was removed. Then, Manoah knew that he had been talking to God Himself.

If people of the Old Testament could be in God's presence and not realize it at first, how much more is it possible for us to be unaware of His presence with us today?

Manoah had seen a *theophany* , a visible appearance or manifestation of God. Perhaps it was a *Christophany, the visible appearance of Christ in a human form.*

In the days of Hezekiah, *the angel of the Lord* appeared to judge the Assyrian army.

> *And it came to pass that night, that **the angel of the Lord** went out, and smote in the camp of the Assyrians an hundred fourscore and five thousand: and when they arose early in the morning, behold, they were all dead corpses.*
>
> 2 Kings 19:35 (KJV)

The manifest presence of God slew an army of mortal beings. What can His presence do today?

David also knew that the presence of God could protect him against any enemy. God's presence puts the enemy to flight. God's presence in your life will repel spiritual darkness that would come against you to destroy you.

David was aware of God's intervention in battle and prayed prophetically concerning his enemies:

> *Let **the angel of the Lord** chase them. Let their way*
> *be dark and slippery: and let **the angel of the Lord***
> *persecute them.*   Psalms 35:5-6 (KJV)

Joshua encountered *the angel of the Lord* as a mighty
warrior:

> *When Joshua was near Jericho, he looked up and saw a*
> *man standing in front of him with a drawn sword in*
> *his hand.*   Joshua 5:13 (NIV)

As happened so many times, Joshua thought the angel
was a man. He looked so much like a man that Joshua
approached him and asked, *"Are you for us of for our enemies?"*

> *"Neither," he replied, "but as commander of the army*
> *of the army of the Lord I have now come."*
>   Verse 14 (NIV)

Angels are warriors. But this was not simply an angelic
warrior. This was the Commander Himself, He Who or-
ders the armies of heaven, He Who gives commands to
the luminaries. At this point, Joshua changed his manner.

> *Then Joshua fell facedown to the ground in reverence,*
> *and asked him, "What message does my Lord have for*
> *his servant?" The commander of the Lord's army re-*
> *plied, "Take off your sandals, for the place where you*
> *are standing is holy." And Joshua did so.*
>   Verses 14-15 (NIV)

Joshua witnessed a *theophany, a representation of the presence of the Lord in a tangible form.* Why was the Son of God appearing in the Old Testament? We can only say that His appearance foreshadowed His coming in the flesh as the Babe in Bethlehem's manger. He has always existed and simply exercised His right to prove that point on these various occasions.

Joshua's response to seeing God was the same as most others who witnessed such an awesome Divine visitation. He fell face down to the ground in a posture of worship.

When Jesus was resurrected from the dead, *the angel of the Lord* was involved.

> *There was a great earthquake: for* **the angel of the Lord** *descended from heaven, and came and rolled back the stone from the door, and sat upon it.*
>
> Matthew 28:2 (KJV)

Could this be the presence of the Divine at the tomb?

> *His countenance was like lightning, and his raiment white as snow: and for fear of him the keepers did shake, and became as dead men.*
>
> Matthew 28:3-4 (KJV)

What an effect the presence of God had on these elite Roman soldiers! They fainted like feeble little old ladies when they were suddenly confronted by the manifest presence of God.

The angel of the Lord delivered Peter and John from prison in Jerusalem.

> *But during the night **an angel of the Lord** opened*
> *the doors of the jail and brought them out. "God stand*
> *in the temple courts," he said, "and tell the people the*
> *full message of this new life."*   Acts 5:19-20 (NIV)

At a later time, Peter was again delivered in a
similar way.

> ***The angel of the Lord** came upon him, and a light*
> *shined in the prison: and he smote Peter on the side,*
> *and raised him up, saying, Arise up quickly. And his*
> *chains fell off from his hands.*   Acts 12:7 (KJV)

The angel of the Lord spoke to Philip, the evangelist,
giving him instructions concerning his immediate
ministry.

> *And **the angel of the Lord** spake unto Philip,*
> *saying, Arise, and go toward the south.*
>   Acts 8:26 (KJV)

In these New Testament cases, it is not as clear that the
Scriptures refer to God. These men saw and spoke with a
celestial creature from the presence of God Yet he is never
referred to as "an angel from the Lord," but always as an
"angel of the Lord." Indeed, at times, the angel in question
looked very much like a man (Mark 16:5).

It is not certain that *the angel of the Lord* in the New
Testament has the same weight as *the angel of the Lord* of
the Old Testament, Who was clearly a manifestation of
God's presence and, in most cases, the preincarnate Christ
Himself.

Other names for *the angel of the Lord*, in Scripture, include *mine angel*, *angel of God*, and *angel of His presence*.

His Manifest Presence as Light

Saul of Tarsus experienced the awesome presence of the Lord on the road to Damascus as a great light. It was the middle of the day, and the sun was probably very intense; yet a greater light overshadowed the sun and blinded him with its intensity.

> *Suddenly **a light** shone around him from heaven. Then he fell to the ground, and heard a voice.*
>
> Acts 9:3-4

Saul was not a believer, and he certainly was not a worshiper; yet the light of the presence of the Lord made him know that God was real. He was, in fact, a persecutor of the Church and a murderer, since he had dedicated his time to helping to deliver Christians to prison and to death. What a miracle of grace that God chose to show the glory of His presence to Saul of Tarsus!

> *"Saul, Saul, why are you persecuting Me? And he said, "Who are You, Lord?" and the Lord said, "I am Jesus, whom you are persecuting." ... So he, trembling and astonished, said, "Lord, what do You want me to do?" And the Lord said to him, "Arise and go into the city, and you will be told what you must do."*
>
> Acts 9:4-6

The presence of Jesus was overwhelming to Saul. When he saw the glory of Jesus, he immediately fell down prostrate, trembling with fear. His traveling companions saw a light and heard a voice but couldn't understand what God was saying. This message was for Saul.

> *The men who journeyed with him stood speechless, hearing a voice but seeing no one.*   Acts 9:7

Apart from the fact that Saul was a rebel who was capturing and tormenting believers, the interesting point here is that Jesus Himself appeared. This was not an ark or a cloud. Jesus was speaking directly to one of His declared enemies.

Once, during a worship seminar in Akron, Ohio, a woman came up to me and said that she had seen a very bright light over my shoulder. She thought her eyes were playing tricks on her, so she blinked repeatedly; but the light would not go away. It could very well have been the manifest presence of the Lord.

The light that came to Saul must have been many times more powerful. It was blinding. Nothing can compare with the glory of the light of God's presence.

His Manifest Presence as a Sound From Heaven and As Tongues of Fire

One of the most well-known portions of scripture in the New Testament concerning the presence of the Lord is found in the book of Acts. As the disciples were waiting in the upper room to receive God's power in their lives,

God's presence was manifested as a great sound, like wind, and as flames of fire.

Jesus had told them to wait in Jerusalem for "*the Promise of the Father.*" In the scriptures the word *Promise* has a capital *P*, because the promise was that God Himself would live in them by His Spirit. He was the Promise.

When they had waited patiently in His presence for ten days, something happened:

> *Suddenly there came **a sound** from heaven, as of a rushing mighty wind, and it filled the whole house where they were sitting. Then there appeared to them divided **tongues, as of fire,** and one sat upon each of them. And they were all filled with the Holy Spirit and began to speak with other tongues, as the Spirit gave them utterance.*   Acts 2:2-4

I find several things about their experience very intriguing. First, it was obvious to the disciples that the sound they heard came from heaven and was not caused by some natural phenomena. The only thing they could liken it to was a "*rushing, mighty wind.*" It must have been like what audio technicians call *white noise, the mixture of all known frequencies, the combination of all the sound waves in the spectrum that we can hear.* What a sound!

Not much is known about the sounds in heaven, but John the Revelator was able to overhear some of them.

> *I heard a voice from heaven, like the voice of many waters and like the voice of loud thunder. And I heard*

> *the sound of harpists playing their harps. And they*
> *sang as it were a new song before the throne.*
>
> Revelation 14:2-3

John described what he heard as *"like the voice of many waters."* This must have been the *white noise* of heaven.

> *I heard, as it were, the voice of a great multitude, as the*
> *sound of many waters and as the sound of mighty*
> *thunderings, saying, "Alleluia! For the Lord God*
> *Omnipotent reigns!"*   Revelation 19:6

Perhaps what John heard was the same sound heard in the upper room on the Day of Pentecost.

Then those present witnessed the flames of fire. The presence of the Lord was both heard and seen that day. Divided flames rested on each of the disciples. God was with them. Everyone knew it.

As a result of this supernatural presence of God, the disciples were filled with the Holy Spirit and began to speak with other languages. When the noise of the joyful disciples' praises was heard in the streets of the city, a large crowd began to gather. The presence of the Lord had an impact on the disciples and, through them, upon the whole city of Jerusalem.

As we have seen, sometimes the presence of God is overwhelming. It is so heavy at times that we feel pressed down by it and must bow our faces to the earth. His presence is penetrating. It is all encompassing. It is so brilliant that none can look upon it. We hide our faces.

One of my most memorable experiences took place at a worship congress in New Orleans. Mardi Gras was in full swing, and people had come from everywhere to celebrate. The streets were filled with drunken revelry.

Inside the conference, we also had reason to rejoice. About twelve hundred Christians attended that night. The place where we met was so crowded that some people were standing along the wall. The worship leader took us to a very special place in the presence of the Lord.

When the songs were finished, there was still a strong, lingering sense of God's presence. The orchestra continued to play very softly as people worshiped.

Before long, we all became aware of something very special that was happening. There was an unusual sense of God's glory and of His holiness. Some people began to weep, and some dropped to their knees before the Lord.

I'll never forget what I saw. I saw men, tall men, most of them pastors, stretched out in a row across the floor in front of the platform. Their faces were pressed down to the carpet, and their arms were stretched out above their heads, palms down.

Although there was no conductor, the musical instruments continued to play. As the Lord gave each musician a melody, he played it. One instrument would crescendo for all to hear, then die down, to blend with the rest; and another would rise.

I remember feeling the weight of God's glory on my body as we waited in His presence. I could no longer remain upright. I simply had to prostrate myself, as others had before me.

Then, for a while, time seemed to stand still as together we touched eternity. Before the throne of the most awesome royalty, we worshiped in the beauty of holiness, the only proper protocol. There was no doubt we were in the manifest presence of God.

Chapter 3

The Promise of His Presence

Lo, I am with you alway, even unto the end of the world. Amen.   Matthew 28:20 (KJV)

The Word of God is full of assurances that God will be with us. Since He is always with us in His omnipresence and it is impossible to hide from Him in any way, this promise is that He will manifest His presence to us. He will allow us to experience a greater dimension of His presence. Although He is with everyone everywhere always, He has promised to show us His presence in unusual ways.

These are the most precious promises of the Bible, for they declare God's willingness to lower Himself to our level and to personally accompany us on our pilgrimage through life.

What a privileged people we are! While the world around us is filled with a terrible sense of loneliness and foreboding, the lowliest saint never need be without the presence of the Creator of the Universe. This is certainly a lesson that many Christians need to learn; for too many have grown accustomed to living without God's personal touch on their daily lives.

His Promise: Collective and Individual

The promise of the Lord's presence is both collective (for us all as God's people) and individual. The Word of God speaks to us as a Body:

> *The angel of the Lord encamps all around those that fear him, and delivers them.* Psalms 34:7

> *As the mountains are round about Jerusalem, so the Lord is round about his people from henceforth even for ever.* Psalms 125:2 (KJV)

> *Then spake Haggai the Lord's messenger in the Lord's message unto the people, saying, I am with you, saith the Lord.* Haggai 1:13 (KJV)

And the Word of God speaks to us as individuals:
When Isaac was forced to leave his lands and go to Beersheba because of his contentious neighbors, the Lord appeared to him that night and assured him:

> *Fear not, for I am with thee.* Genesis 26:24 (KJV)

God promised Moses that he would not walk alone when he went back to Egypt to confront the evil Pharaoh.

The God of the universe would go with him and help him every step of the way.

Certainly, I will be with thee.   Exodus 3:12 (KJV)

When Moses died, God promised Joshua that He would accompany him, as He had Moses.

When faced with the challenge of rebuilding the temple, after the return of the exiles, in the days of the prophet Haggai, God spoke very clearly to those in charge:

Yet now be strong, O Zerubbabel, saith the Lord; and be strong, O Joshua, son of Josedech, the high priest; and be strong, all ye people of the land, saith the Lord, and work: for I am with you, saith the Lord of hosts.
Haggai 2:4 (KJV)

Dozens of Bible characters received similar promises, and those promises are recorded for our encouragement. God is with us as individuals, whatever our particular situation in life.

Often, God manifests His presence to us in times of danger or trouble.

Be not afraid of the king of Babylon, of whom ye are afraid; be not afraid of him, saith the Lord: for I am with you to save you, and to deliver you from his hand.   Jeremiah 42:11 (KJV)

And when God does manifest His presence, the situation changes.

For the Lord your God in your midst, the Mighty One, will save.
I will deal with all who afflict you; I will save the lame.
Zephaniah 3:17 & 19

Our cry to God must be, as David said:

Be not far from me; for trouble is near.
Psalms 22:11 (KJV)

Nothing could give us more comfort and encouragement than to read and believe the promises of God's manifest presence with His people.

These promises were not just for Jeremiah, David and Zerubbabel. They are for every saint to appropriate. God is with us to help us with all of life's trials.

God has promised to accompany us on our journey of life, giving to us freely the benefits of His fellowship, His care, His provision and His strength.

God is our fortress. In Him, we find safety. He is our protection, our sanctuary — not in an ethereal or abstract sense, but in reality. This is not a theological concept. This is a tangible blessing.

God is our rest in the midst of the turmoil of life. He is with us in battle. He goes before us to utter His voice before His army. When we go to war against principalities and powers, He is always present with us to preserve and protect His beloved.

He is always with us.

When Judah had to go out to war against backslidden Israel, Abijah comforted and encouraged the people with theses powerful words:

God himself is with us for our captain.
> 2 Chronicles 13:12 (KJV)

When the Assyrians, under the famous Sennacherib, invaded Judah and threatened to destroy the city of Jerusalem, Hezekiah took courage and spoke to his captains:

With us is the Lord our God.
> 2 Chronicles 32:8 (KJV)

In both cases, Judah miraculously prevailed in battle. How could they lose — when God was on their side?

We are so precious to the Lord that He uses the most intimate terms of endearment when speaking of us in His Word.

I am with thee.
I will hold thy ... hand.
> Isaiah 41:10 & 13 (KJV)

Paul knew this nurturing of an ever present and loving God.

The Lord stood with me, and strengthened me.
> 2 Timothy 4:17 (KJV)

The Lord of heaven and of earth is with us, not only to preserve us, but to display His power in our behalf. He is with us as Guide, to direct our steps; He is with us as

Counsellor, to instruct us; He is with us as Friend, to comfort our hearts; and He is with us as Savior, to free us from sin.

This promise of God's presence is the predominant theme of scripture. This is the purpose of God. He has always manifested His presence to His people, and He always will.

The promises of Divine presence with us should bring tremendous stability and strength to every Christian. Earthly friends fail us, but God is faithful. His presence is constant. He doesn't change His mind, break His promise, or withdraw from us — as others do.

Being deprived of human companionship often does bring loneliness. The loss of a mate or a child or a close friend are among the most serious emotional traumas that we face in life. The Lord God of Heaven and Earth says to all those who are lonely:

I will never leave thee, nor forsake thee.
Hebrews 13:5 (KJV)

Life has its difficult moments for each of us. This is not an easy journey on which we are embarked. But the promise of God's presence with us makes it all worthwhile. He is with us everywhere and always, by His omnipresence. And He has promised to manifest His presence to us in a real and tangible way. We are blessed with a double portion of His presence in our lives.

Others may forsake us, but there is always Someone who is willing to accompany us, to make us recipients of His fellowship, His care, His provision, and His strength.

This promise of God's presence with His children has longevity. He has promised to be with us *unto the end of the world* or *unto the end of the age*. No matter when we are in need of Him, no matter how often, or how long, He is there for us.

Even in gross darkness, He is there to light the way. If the darkness is *the shadow of death*, He is present to hold and comfort us.

> *Yea, though I walk through the valley of the shadow of death, I will fear no evil: for thou art with me; thy rod and thy staff they comfort me.* Psalms 23:4 (KJV)

There is nothing more certain in a Christian's life than the promise of God's presence. He never fails. He will perform His Word.

Are we not honored to be favored with such an illustrious presence? Such promises should release us from fear and loneliness and should empower us to witness. Because of the multiple benefits the assurance of His presence have for us, we should each take time to cultivate His presence and the realization of His presence in our daily lives.

His Promise to Be With Us as *the Lord of Hosts*

The phrase *the Lord of Hosts* is a military term meaning *the Lord or captain of armies*. The word *hosts* refers to *a mass of persons, especially organized for war (an army), a campaign, company, soldiers, ready for war*.

The name *Lord of Hosts* is a technical term signifying *Yahweh, the mightiest warrior, or Yahweh, the all powerful King*. The name affirms God's universal rulership that encompasses every force or army, whether heavenly or earthly. The name points to Jehovah of Hosts, the Lord Almighty, the King of Glory.

It is His throne name, His royal name.

> *I saw also the Lord sitting upon a throne, high and lifted up, and His train filled the temple. Above it stood the seraphim ... . And one cried unto another, and said, Holy, holy, holy, is the Lord of hosts: the whole earth is full of His glory.*   Isaiah 6:1-3 (KJV)

This name was associated with the Ark of the Covenant, where God was believed to maintain His throne.

> *David arose, and went ... to bring up ... the ark of God, whose name is called by the name of the Lord of hosts that dwelleth between the cherubims.*
>   2 Samuel 6:2 (KJV)

The *Lord of Hosts* was manifested in Shiloh.

> *This man went up out of his city yearly to worship and to sacrifice unto the Lord of hosts in Shiloh.*
>   1 Samuel 1:3 (KJV)

Shiloh was special because God's presence was manifest there visibly above the Ark of the Covenant, between the golden cherubim. Those who went there were aware of approaching *"the Lord of hosts"* — the all powerful Lord of mighty armies.

This name, *the Lord of hosts*, is also the name associated with God's glory. It is related to His shekinah.

> *So the people sent to Shiloh, that they might bring from thence the ark of the covenant of **the Lord of hosts**, which dwelleth between the cherubims.*
>
> 1 Samuel 4:4 (KJV)

When the people stood before the Ark, they could sense the power of the Lord of all armies. David used that name to defeat the giant Goliath.

> *Then said David to the Philistine, "You come to me with a sword, with a spear, and with a javelin. But I come to you in the name of **the Lord of hosts**, the God of the armies of Israel, whom you have defied.*
>
> 1 Samuel 17:45 (KJV)

Poor Goliath! He may have been big in stature, but he was no match for the Lord of all armies, the mightiest conqueror in heaven and earth. He laughed, thinking that he was facing a mere boy; but he perished when he came face to face with the power of the presence of *the Lord of hosts*.

Watch out, enemies of God! When *the Lord of Hosts* stirs His armies for battle, you have no chance.

> *The noise of a multitude in the mountains, like as of a great people: a tumultuous noise of the kingdoms of*

nations gathered together: the Lord of hosts mus-
tereth the host of the battle.   Isaiah 13:4 (KJV)

One certainly doesn't want to be on the opposite side of
this Mightiest of Warriors. The wrath of *the Lord of Hosts* is
nothing to scoff at.

Therefore I will shake the heavens, and the earth shall
*remove out of her place, in the wrath of **the Lord of***
***hosts**, and in the day of His fierce anger.*
                                             Isaiah 13:13 (KJV)

There is also ability to bless in that powerful name.

As soon as David had made an end of offering burnt
offerings and peace offerings, he blessed the people in
*the name of **the Lord of hosts**.*
                                          2 Samuel 6:18 (KJV)

There is a zeal in this name.

For out of Jerusalem shall go forth a remnant, and
*they that escape out of mount Zion: the zeal of **the***
***Lord of hosts** shall do this.*   2 Kings 19:31 (KJV)

God has promised that the power and authority of this,
our mighty Champion, is present to keep us safe.

***The Lord of hosts** is with us; the God of Jacob is our*
refuge. Selah   Psalms 46:7 (KJV)

Our God will manifest Himself in wise counsel for His children.

> *This also comes forth from **the Lord of hosts**, which is wonderful in counsel, and excellent in working.*
> Isaiah 28:29 (KJV)

The promise of His presence in the future, as *the Lord of hosts*, can be found throughout Scripture.

> *Then ... **the Lord of hosts** shall reign in mount Zion, and in Jerusalem, and before His ancients gloriously.*
> Isaiah 24:23 (KJV)

> *Yea, many people and strong nations shall come to seek **the Lord of hosts** in Jerusalem, and to pray before the Lord.*
> Zechariah 8:22 (KJV)

His Promise to Be With Us as *Immanuel*

God's promise of companionship is revealed in still another name given to the Lord: *Immanuel*, which means *God is with us*. The rich revelation given to Isaiah of the presence of God with His people, included this name, *Immanuel*.

> *Therefore the Lord himself shall give you a sign; Behold, a virgin shall conceive, and bear a son, and shall call his name **Immanuel**.*
> Isaiah 7:14 (KJV)

Matthew saw Immanuel (or Emmanuel) from the other end, the fulfillment of the prophecy of Isaiah — when Jesus came to earth as a man. He quoted Isaiah:

*Behold, a virgin shall be with child, and shall bring
forth a son, and they shall call his name **Emmanuel**,
which being interpreted is, God with us.*

Matthew 1:23 (KJV)

What a promise! Almighty God is with us. His presence
was manifested in human flesh as the Christ child. But He
yet makes Himself available to those who love Him. He is
still Emmanuel. He is still *God with us.* We can experience
His presence anytime we have need to do so.

He is not only with us (and in us) at the moment when
we accept Him as our Lord and Savior. He wants to manifest Himself to us often, giving us a constant awareness of
His nearness.

His Promise to Be With Us
in the Completion of the Great Commission

These promises are neither outdated or irrelevant to our
daily lives. They are just as true today as they were in
David's time. God is just as much present to deliver us
from our giants as He was to deliver the young David
from Goliath.

Jesus included a promise of His abiding presence with
the great commission He gave to His disciples before He
left them.

*Go ye therefore, and teach all nations, baptizing them
in the name of the Father, and of the Son, and of the
Holy Ghost: Teaching them to observe all things
whatsoever I have commanded you: and, **lo, I am***

> *with you alway, even unto the end of the*
> *world. Amen*   Matthew 28:20 (KJV)

The Lord of the harvest will be with us, even to the end of the age. Then, when the age is finished, we will be with Him FOREVER. Throughout eternity, our knowledge of God will increase, and we will know Him in a much greater way.

> *For now we see through a glass, darkly; but then face*
> *to face: now I know in part; but then shall I know even*
> *as also I am known.*   1 Corinthians 13:12 (KJV)

Someday we will know the Lord in a much more intimate dimension. We will understand what Moses experienced when he saw God *face to face*. No matter how glorious the dimension of His manifest presence has been to us here on the earth, greater things await us — in His ultimate presence.

In the meantime, we will continue to do His will, having the assurance that He is with us at every moment of every day, and that we have nothing to fear. We believe His promise that as we go forth to make His name known to the ends of the earth, He is always with us. He will never forsake us. This is the promise of His omnipresence presence and could be of His manifest presence, if we abide in it.

Chapter 4

The Men of His Presence

Not every man in Bible history had a personal quest for the presence of God, but those who loved Him did. These were individuals who desired the presence of God more than anything else in life and who learned to experience and live in His manifest presence. To show the contrast, I include a few people who rejected God's presence and suffered the consequences.

Adam

So God created man in his own image, in the image of God he created him; male and female he created them. And God blessed them and said to them, Be fruitful.
Genesis 1:27-28 (KJV)

Adam and Eve were the first to experience the peace and blessing of the Creator's presence with man. Because of that, they became the target of Satan's deceit. He hated God and had become His enemy; therefore, he automatically became the enemy of those whom God loved and favored. He would not rest night or day from trying to destroy the beauty that God had invested in Adam and Eve and devised a scheme to make them lose confidence in God's Word and disobey and disappoint Him. He was *"cunning."*

> *Now the serpent was more cunning than any beast of the field which the Lord God had made. And He said to the woman, "Has God indeed said, 'Your shall not eat of every tree of the garden'?"*   Genesis 3:1

The serpent knew that if he could entice man to go against God's express commands, he could break the bond of fellowship that existed between them. He challenged what God had said by putting his private interpretation on it. His interpretation was misleading and changed the meaning of God's words.

> *And the serpent said to the woman, "You will not surely die. For God knows that in the day you eat of it your eyes will be opened, and you will be like God, knowing good and evil."*   Genesis 3:4-5

Despite the fact that the serpent was directly contradicting God, he did it in such a manner that it sounded reasonable, and Eve was seduced by his words. She had not yet learned that fellowship with the Lord demands a quick and cheerful response to His voice.

After Adam and Eve became conscience of their sin, they suddenly realized that they were now deprived of the benefits of God's presence, benefits they had enjoyed in the garden. Sin has always separate men from the presence of the Lord. Disobedience to God and His Word becomes a barrier to fellowship with Him. Sin will always come between you and your Maker — if it is not quickly dealt with and resolved.

What a shock it must have been for Adam and Eve when they found themselves locked out of the garden and locked out of the blessing of God for their lives! They had not known what it was to be without His presence. Created in His manifest presence, they had daily lived and breathed in the revealed essence of the Lord God. Now, not only had their lives been turned upside down, but there was another presence in their lives. This new presence constantly competed for their attention and separated them from the Lord and His presence. Satan will do ANYTHING to get between a man and his God.

The tactic of the serpent was to get the eyes of Adam and his wife off the Lord and His Word and to get their eyes on self-gratification, self-fulfillment, selfishness and self-seeking. Anytime we put our own interests above the Lord and His will for us, we are in jeopardy of losing the presence of God. The moment we become self-seeking, sin will shortly follow and will alienate us from God's precious presence.

> *So when the woman saw that the tree was good for food, that it was pleasant to the eyes, and a tree*

desirable to make one wise, she took of its fruit and ate.
She also gave to her husband with her, and he ate.

Genesis 3:6

What a surprise when they realized that this decision placed them into another dimension, disconnected from Father's presence! The sin of disobedience had done it's horrendous work. No longer did the presence of the Lord cover their lives and warm their hearts with the sense of His nearness.

Then the eyes of both of them were opened, and they
knew that they were naked; and they sewed fig leaves
together and made themselves coverings.

Genesis 3:7

For the first time, the man and the woman felt shame; and they felt fear, fear of God, fear of His presence. What had been to them, until that day, cause for rejoicing now became cause for alarm. What would God think? What would He say? What would He do? When they heard Him in the garden, instead of running to Him — as they had done before — they hid themselves.

And they heard the sound [voice] *of the Lord God*
walking in the garden in the cool of the day, and
Adam and his wife hid themselves from the presence of
the Lord God among the trees of the garden.

Genesis 3:8

What a horrible thing it was for them to be alienated from the Lord! They had been the most intimate of friends, so close was their fellowship. Now they were willing to identify more with sin and to avoid God's presence.

His approaching footsteps must have roared like thunder in their ears. Then, they heard His comforting voice, wafting on the evening breeze. He was calling them. But this time something seemed to be different about His voice. To them, it was no longer comforting; it was terrifying. They crouched in the shadows, hoping against hope that He would not detect their presence and would go away and leave them alone.

Adam and Eve knew nothing of repentance and of Father's willingness to offer complete forgiveness. They knew nothing yet of God's Lamb, sacrificed to take our place. They did not yet know how to make a blood offering. They were caught in a trap with no way of escape. Sin isolated them from Father, and they saw no way to get back to Him. They must hide themselves and hope that He would not find them.

How foolish they were! God is everywhere. Nothing is hidden from His sight. Nothing is kept from His knowledge. No one can avoid Him. It is impossible to hide from God.

Adam and Eve were not hiding from the omnipresence of God. They were avoiding a personal encounter with Him. They were avoiding His revealed presence.

God felt the loss of Adam's fellowship and of Eve's fellowship as much as Adam and Eve felt their loss of God's benefits. God wants friends. He wants companions. He was not willing to slip out of the garden and leave man hiding in the bushes. He called to Adam.

> *Then the Lord God called to Adam and said to him,*
> *"Where are you?"*   Genesis 3:9

God knew where Adam was. He knows everything. He is present with everything and everyone. He was asking why Adam was not rushing to meet Him. Why he was not eager to see Him? Why he was no longer with Him? Why he was hiding from Him?

Adam had always welcomed God's presence and delighted in their times together. His absence was a clear indication that something was wrong. Hiding from God was not normal behavior. God's question was an invitation to confession or repentance. He knew where Adam was; but was Adam willing to recognize that he had fallen?

Adam replied:

> *"I heard Your voice in the garden, and I was afraid*
> *because I was naked; and I hid myself."*
>   Genesis 3:10

Adam was now self-conscious, concerned with how he looked in the presence of God. That hadn't concerned him before. Sin makes you uncomfortable in the presence of God, it makes you self-conscience instead of God-conscience.

Adam attributed his fear to the wrong cause. He blamed his fear on his lack of clothing, not on his discomfort in the presence of the Creator. He was more conscience of the effects of his sin than of the sin itself. Sin confuses people. Not only does it deceive us and rob us of His presence, it leaves our thinking muddled.

> *Therefore the Lord God sent him out of the garden of Eden to till the ground from which he was taken. So He drove out the man; and He placed cherubim at the east of the garden of Eden, and a flaming sword which turned every way, to guard the way to the tree of life.*
> Genesis 3:23-24

Justice demanded that Adam leave the garden God had prepared for him and that he begin earning his keep by plowing and planting the soil, now cursed because of his sin. That day the curse came upon man, upon woman, upon the beasts and upon the land.

The greatest result of Adam's sin, however, was separation from God's presence. Intimacy and fellowship with the Divine was broken. The barrenness of man's new surroundings spoke of the barrenness of his relationship with his Creator, a relationship that was once as fertile as the garden in which God had lovingly placed him.

Mighty cherubs, angelic ministers of God, were positioned at the east end of the garden to keep Adam from the tree of life and from the presence of God. Cherubs were glorious creatures with either four or six wings (Ezekiel 1:8, 2:23, 10:7, Revelation 4:8). Each cherub had four faces and they were *"full of eyes."* In the Apocalypse, they are seen standing in the immediate area of the throne of God, adoring and praising the Eternal One.

After the fall, cherubs were ordered to stand guard at Eden's gate to prevent Adam from returning to the tree of life and to the presence of God. By this act, God was trying to say that only when purified and redeemed could fallen man return to His presence. Meanwhile, man was unfit to enter this resplendent abode.

With the cherubs (two or more) was a flaming sword that turned constantly. The sword was a separate existence, very much like a Divine presence, moving, guarding, watching over the access to the tree of life and the manifest presence of Life.

Adam could not return to the garden. The glory and beauty of the Lord's presence became a memory, and man was shunned, a fugitive, cursed to dwell far from his Father who gave him life.

Enoch

Enoch walked with God 300 years and had other sons and daughters. Altogether, Enoch lived 365 years. Enoch walked with God; then he was no more because God took him away.   Genesis 5:22-24 (NIV)

Enoch was the son of Jared, a descendant of Adam through Seth. He is better known as the father of Methuselah (the oldest man in the Bible) and one of only two men in the Old Testament who did not taste death. *God took him away.*

Enoch experienced a unique departure because he had live uniquely on the earth. He walked with God for three hundred years. I wish we could live to be three hundred years old so that we could walk with the Lord as long as Enoch did.

The word *walked* is intriguing here. It means *the going, movement or way of man*, like the *creeping* of a snake, or the *prowling* of foxes, or the *flowing* of water. It could mean *the procession of man* or, in a general sense, *the journey of man through life*. It speaks of the continuity of the action or movement. Enoch developed a life-style of walking with God.

Enoch walked *with* God. He was near God, close to God. Enoch knew the manifest presence of God in his life. The two of them, Enoch and God, walked together. God walked and Enoch walked, but they did it together. They had communion and fellowship with each other. They had an intimate relationship. Enoch lived in the presence of the Lord.

> *It was because of his faith that Enoch was taken up and did not have to experience death: he was not to be found because God had taken him.*
> Hebrews 11:5 (The Jerusalem Bible)

Another translation says that he was taken up to God, or to heaven. All this happened because of Enoch's faith in what God said.

Faith is exercised toward an object. We have faith in something or somebody. As Christians, we must have faith in God and in what He has said. This is the faith that gives substance to the things we hope for and certainty to the things we don't yet see.

As Enoch walked with God, they communicated with each other. Enoch talked with God, and God talked with Enoch. When God told him something, Enoch believed it.

Intimacy produces this type of confidence. Enoch had faith because he walked with God. He believed God because he knew God intimately.

We don't know all that God told Enoch. Did He tell him that he would not die? Perhaps. But whatever God told him, Enoch believed. And because he believed, he experienced what God had promised him.

> *It was because of his faith that Enoch was taken to the eternal world without experiencing death.*
>
> Hebrews 11:5 (Phillips)

Enoch was *"translated."* God picked him up and carried him away to an eternal dimension. In this way, God revealed His presence to Enoch in a special way.

The challenge we receive from the life of Enoch is two-fold: to walk with God and to believe what He says. To walk with God is to spend time in His presence, to live in a constant state of God-consciousness, to commune and fellowship with Him on a regular basis, to be where He is and to get to know Him.

To walk by faith is to enter another dimension in which we are motivated, not by the circumstances around us, but by what God says.

Many of us have experienced being caught up into a higher dimension, in which we were totally oblivious to the natural realm. For a time, we lost all awareness of time and space, so that hours in His presence seemed like only a few minutes, as we communed with Him beyond the veil of the natural perception. This is only a taste of what God has prepared for us.

Job

In the land of Uz there lived a man whose name was Job. This man was blameless and upright; he feared God and shunned evil.

Job 1:1 (NIV)

Job was a man of God's presence. Those around him envied him because of his intimate relationship with God and the very apparent blessing of God upon his large family, his many lands, his bountiful crops, his numerous animals, and his many workers.

Things did not always go well for Job. One day a servant came to tell him that the Sabeans, his enemies, had stolen his oxen and his donkeys.

Before the first servant had finished his sad report, another appeared to announce that fire had mysteriously fallen from heaven and burned up all his sheep and the servants who cared for them.

Before the second servant had finished, another appeared to give his account: that the Chaldeans, in three raiding parties, had swept down upon Job's camels and *"carried them off,"* killing the servants who kept them.

The final message that came that day was the worst: while Job's sons and daughters had been gathered for a feast at the elder brother's house, a strong wind had come up unexpectedly, destroying the house, and killing all ten children.

What Job did that day should challenge every one of us. He arose and worshiped God.

Then Job arose and tore his robe and shaved his head,
and he fell to the ground and worshiped. And he said:
"Naked I came from my mother's womb
And naked shall I return there.
The Lord gave, and the Lord has taken away;
Blessed be the name of the Lord."
In all this Job did not sin nor charge God with wrong.
                                                              Job 1:20-22

Job was a worshiper — on bad days as well as good days. He knew God; and he knew that God doesn't change. He is always the same — no matter what happens today. Job loved God and knew that God loved him. He trusted God to always look out for his interests. This all came about through Job's passion for God's presence. He loved to be with God, and He loved to speak with God. The Bible records lengthy conversations between Job and his God (Chapters 38-42.).

Nothing can replace an intimate relationship with the Lord. Job was on talking terms with God. He treasured the manifestation of the presence of God in his life.

With a relationship like that, Job could not lose. He had to go up. He could not go down. He had to win. He could not lose. He had to prosper. He could not remain in want.

The Lord restored Job's losses when he prayed for his
friends. Indeed the Lord gave Job twice as much as he
had before.
The Lord blessed the latter days of Job more than his
beginning.   Job 42:10 & 12

Abraham

The Lord had said to Abram, "Leave your country, your people and your father's household and go the land I will show you. I will make you into a great nation and I will bless you."

Genesis 12:1-2 (NIV)

The name *Abraham*, given by God to Abram (an Aramean and descendant of Shem), means *father of a multitude*. Abraham is revered as the father of all Jews and Christians and the first of the great patriarchs.

God chose Abraham as the man through whom He wanted to bless all mankind and called him to a unique walk of faith. He would leave his own land and his father's family and would travel toward a new land which God would show him. In that new place God would raise up, from Abraham's loins, a new nation to serve Him.

But to get to this new place, Abraham would need to cross three hundred miles of hostile territory. And once he arrived in Canaan, he would wander with his family for many years as a nomad, in search of food and water for the flocks they kept.

As a foreigner, Abraham was not permitted to own land or to build a permanent dwelling, very difficult for a man who was accustomed to prosperity in his home land. His willingness to obey God in these difficult circumstances has been praised by every succeeding generation as an example of faith. Abraham believed God.

And the scripture was fulfilled which saith, Abraham
believed God, and it was imputed unto him for righ-
teousness: and he was called the friend of God.
                                    James 2:23 (KJV)

Abraham's unquestioning faith was a result of his intimate relationship with God. He and God often had
conversations. Because they were close, God could trust
Abraham with His plan.

So Abram left, as the Lord had told him.
The Lord appeared to Abram *and said, "To your*
offspring I will give this land." So he built an altar
there to the Lord, who had appeared to him.
                                    Genesis 12:4 & 7 (NIV)

At every juncture of his life, God was there to speak to
Abraham just what he needed to hear at the moment. The
manifestation of God's presence was, to Abraham,
awesome.

The Lord appeared to him and said, "I am God Al-
mighty, walk before me and be blameless."
Abram fell facedown.   Genesis 17:1 & 3 (NIV)

Sometimes God appeared to Abraham in visions (Genesis 15:1-3); sometimes Abraham heard the audible voice
of God (Verses 13 & 18); and sometimes the manifestation
of God's presence to Abraham was very unusual.

The Lord said to him, "Bring me a heifer, a goat and a
ram, each three years old, along with a dove and a

young pigeon." Abraham brought all these to him, cut them in two and arranged the halves opposite each other; the birds, however, he did not cut in half.
As the sun was setting, Abram fell into a deep sleep, and a thick and dreadful darkness came over him.
*When the sun had set and darkness had fallen, **a smoking firepot with a blazing torch appeared and passed between the pieces.** On that day the Lord made a covenant with Abram.*

Genesis 15:9-10, 12 & 17-18 (NIV)

A dark, heavy cloud or darkness came over Abraham as he slept. This could very possibly have been a manifestation of the presence of God. Then a pot of fire and smoke and a blazing torch moved between the pieces of the sacrifice Abraham had made. Were the fiery pot and the torch manifestations of God's presence in confirmation of the pact He and Abraham were making?

__The Lord appeared__ to Abraham near the great trees of Mamre while he was sitting at the entrance to his tent in the heat of the day. Abraham looked up and saw three men standing nearby. When he saw them, he hurried from the entrance of his tent to meet them and bowed low to the ground. Genesis 18:1-2 (NIV)

On this occasion, God appeared to Abraham as a human visitor, a very unusual manifestation of His presence. With Him were two angels, also in human form. It is not clear whether Abraham immediately recognized that he was talking with God. But very quickly the nature of his visitors became evident. This visitor knew the name of Abraham's wife and knew the fact that she was barren.

> *Then the Lord said, "I will surely return to you about this time next year, and Sarah your wife will have a son."*   Genesis 18:10 (NIV)

Abraham's Visitor was God Himself. The Scriptures call Him *"the Lord,"* and what He proposed was clearly impossible — in human terms. He said that Sarah would become pregnant, when she was already too old to have children.

God could have sent an angel to speak with Abraham. He could have given him a dream or a vision. He could have sent a prophet. On this occasion, however, He decided to take the message personally, to appear to Abraham as a man.

Many people have seen God and talked to God in visions. But Abraham had the privilege of sitting down with God around a Bedouin table and having a conversation over lunch. God ate with him. This clearly was not a vision but a more tangible evidence of God's presence.

> *When the men got up to leave, they looked down toward Sodom, and Abraham walked along with them to see them on their way. Then the Lord said, "Shall I hide from Abraham what I am about to do?"*
> *Then the Lord said, "The outcry of Sodom and Gomorrah is so great and their sin so grievous that I*

> *will go down and see if what they have done is as bad*
> *as the outcry that has reached me. If not I will know."*
> Genesis 18:16-17 & 20-21 (NIV)

The Lord intended to *"go down"* to Sodom. You might say that He wanted to personally "check it out." His omnipresence is everywhere; He monitors everything; and He knows everything. Here, however, He indicated a desire to have a closer look. He wanted to reveal His personage among the filth of Sodom and Gomorrah.

> *The men turned away and went toward Sodom, but*
> *Abraham remained **standing before the Lord**. Then*
> *Abraham approached him.*
> Genesis 18:22-23 (NIV)

God told Abraham about the sin of Sodom and Gomorrah and what He intended to do with the people there because He knew that Abraham was a man of intercession. And Abraham interceded for the inhabitants of those two cities.

The two angels went to Sodom. There they accepted the hospitality of Lot and the protection of his home. When the wicked men of Sodom knew that Lot had guests (and these angels must have been tall, good-looking, fellows), they demanded that he release them, presuming them to be normal men, whom they could abuse. The men of Sodom were homosexuals and wanted to engage in sexual perversion with the visitors. (This is why the practice of homosexuality has, since then, been called "sodomy," and those who practice it, "sodomites.")

Sodom had become so morally depraved that its men had nothing better to do than abuse visitors. These men didn't ask Lot if they could speak to his guests. They demanded that he release them into their hands. What terrible lust! These men burned with desire to fulfill their sexual fantasies. They were addicted to their sin.

Lot did not consent to these demands. Apparently, he had not been contaminated by the evils of Sodom — in that way. He was not, however, without spot, for he suggested that they take his daughters instead. Whether Lot thought he was doing a good thing, in protecting his visitors and allowing "a lesser evil," we cannot say. What we can say is that you simply cannot live that close to sin and not be affected.

God was ready to manifest His glory in Sodom. He can handle sin. It presents no problem for Him. He went there to offer His presence, but the people of Sodom were totally absorbed in their lust. Don't limit God. He is willing to manifest His presence anywhere to anyone, when there is the possibility that men and women may turn to Him.

The angels had to grab Lot and pull him back into his house. His neighbors, denied the privilege of violating the visitors, were attempting to physically drag him away. The crowd was not happy with the action of the visitors and attempted to tear down the door of the house. To prevent further violence, the angels struck these men blind, and they were unable to find the door.

God had offered His presence to the people of Sodom. The fact that they had reacted in such a vile manner only proved the inevitable: Sodom must be destroyed. The angels said:

*"The outcry to the Lord against its people is so great
that he has sent us to destroy it."*
                                                    Genesis 19:13 (NIV)

And soon the destruction of the city began.

*Then the Lord rained down burning sulfur on Sodom
and Gomorrah — from the Lord out of the heavens.*
                                                    Genesis 19:24 (NIV)

Unless God's presence among sinners produces repentance and confession of sin, the final outcome will always
be judgement. The burning sulfur came from the Lord's
presence.

Jacob

*When he reached a certain place, he stopped for the
night because the sun had set. Taking one of the stones
there, he put it under his head and lay down to sleep.
He had a dream in which he saw a stairway resting on
the earth, with its top reaching to heaven, and the
angels of God were ascending and descending on it.
There above it **stood the Lord,** and he said; "I am the
Lord, the God of your father Abraham and the God of
Isaac."
"I am with you and will watch over you wherever you
go, and I will bring you back to this land. I will not
leave you until I have done what I have promised
you."*

When Jacob awoke from his sleep, he thought, "Surely the Lord is in this place, and I was not aware of it." He was afraid and said, "How awesome is this place! This is none other than the house of God; this is the gate of heaven."   Genesis 28:11-13 & 15-17 (NIV)

When Jacob woke up, he recognized that he had witnessed a portal opening to the very presence of God, a stairway with one end touching earth and the other extending into heaven. At the top of the stairway stood God Himself. He was not sitting on His throne, as He normally did. He was standing.

I can somehow visualize that scene. I see the Lord with His hands outstretched toward the stairs, inviting mankind to come into His manifest presence.

Angels were going up the ladder into the presence of God and coming down the ladder from the presence of God. They were entering and exiting God's presence, bringing the glory of His manifest presence with them. Jacob called this *the gate of heaven.*

Few people have ever seen what Jacob saw that day, the entrance to heaven. Many have seen the Lord and many have seen angels. But few have seen them in this way. What he saw left him in awe. He said, *"Surely the Lord is in this place, and I was not aware of it."* Jacob, the son of Isaac, the son of Abraham, had experienced the manifest presence of God.

Early the next morning Jacob took the stone he had placed under his head and set it up as a pillar and poured oil on top of it. He called that place Bethel.

> *Then Jacob made a vow, saying, ... "This stone that I*
> *have set up as a pillar will be God's house."*
> Genesis 28:18-22 (NIV)

Jacob called that place *Bethel, house of God*. He had never seen God in this way before. He had never experienced His presence so strongly. Surely God must live in this place. This must be His house — *Bethel*.

The strange thing about this encounter is that Jacob was not seeking God. He was on a journey to seek a wife. But God was seeking Jacob. He had chosen him to continue the godly line, to pass on the faith of his fathers, Abraham and Isaac, and to become Israel, the nation God had ordained through Abram.

This encounter frightened Jacob. He was not totally comfortable in the presence of God. But he made a vow that day: if God would help him on his journey and would cause him to return safely, he would serve Him.

Many years would pass before Jacob returned to his own land. During that time, he lived with his uncle Laban and served him for his daughters. By the time he returned to his homeland, he had two wives, eleven sons and a great herd of cattle. As he camped one night along the way, he had another strange experience, another Divine encounter.

> *So Jacob was left alone, and a Man wrestled with him*
> *till daybreak. When the Man saw that He could not*
> *overpower him, He touched the socket of Jacob's hip so*
> *that his hip was wrenched as he wrestled with the*

Man. Then the Man said, "Let Me go, for it is daybreak."

But Jacob replied, "I will not let you go unless you bless me."

The Man asked him, "What is your name? "

"Jacob," he answered.

*Then the Man said, "Your name will no longer be Jacob, but Israel, because **you have struggled with God** and with men and have overcome."*

Then He blessed him there.

*So Jacob called the place Peniel, saying, "It is because **I saw God face to face,** and yet my life was spared."*

Genesis 32:24-28 & 29-30 (NIV)

The passage raises many questions, among them: Who was this man? Was this the Lord God Jehovah? Or was this the preincarnate Logos, the Christ? If it was the presence of the Divine, why could He not overpower Jacob? Why did the Man say, let Me go? Why couldn't He break away from Jacob?

What is certain is that Jacob had met with God. *Peniel* means *face of God*. Jacob knew that he had wrestled with God Himself, had been face to face in a most intimate encounter. And he would never be the same again. He was changed for life. His flesh was permanently marked where the Lord had touched him, and he limped, probably for the rest of his life.

The sun rose above him as he passed Peniel, and he was limping because of his hip. Therefore to this day the Israelites do not eat the tendon attached to the socket of the hip, because the socket of Jacob's hip was touched near the tendon. Genesis 32:31-32 (NIV)

Jacob carried a visible mark from being in the presence of God. His was much different from the mark Cain wore, banishing him from God's presence and making him a fugitive in the earth. Jacob's mark was just the opposite. He was marked *for* God's presence. From that night on Jacob's life was different because Jacob was different. The presence of God will change our lives — if we let it.

But we all, with open face, beholding ... the glory of the Lord, are changed into the same image from glory to glory, even as by the Spirit of the Lord.
2 Corinthians 3:18 (KJV)

Moses

"I will send My Angel before you, and I will drive out the Canaanite and the Amorite and Hittite and the Perizzite and Hivite and the Jebusite. Go up to a land flowing with milk and honey."

Exodus 33:2-3

The fact that Moses was one of the greatest men of the Bible, without a doubt, is due to the fact that he spent so much time in the presence of God. Moses loved God's presence.

After he had met God face to face at the burning bush, Moses took advantage of every opportunity to commune with God and experience Him intimately. He talked to God in the glory on Mount Sinai. He talked to God in the tent of meeting.

> *Moses took his tent and pitched it outside the camp, far from the camp, and called it the tabernacle of meeting. And it came to pass that everyone who sought the Lord went out to the tabernacle of meeting which was outside the camp.*   Exodus 33:7

Moses did whatever was necessary — no effort was too great — so that he and all Israel could seek the Lord. He was not afraid to withdraw himself from the crowd if it was necessary. If a special tent was necessary, he would make a special tent. The tent which Moses made, "the tent of meeting," became such a blessing to the children of Israel. It turned their lives around.

> *So it was, whenever Moses went out to the tabernacle, that all the people rose, and each man stood at his tent door and watched Moses until he had gone into the tabernacle. And it came to pass, when Moses entered the tabernacle, that the pillar of cloud descended and stood at the door of the tabernacle, and **the Lord talked with Moses.***   Exodus 33:8-9

The people loved to see Moses go to the tent. It was an exciting moment for them. They were expecting to see God work in some way. God did miracles when His people sought Him.

But, instead of watching Moses, they should have gone in themselves and talked with God face to face. Many Christians love to see miracles. They love to see other people get healed. They enjoy watching other people fall in the Spirit. But they don't draw near to God themselves. They would seemingly rather watch the phenomena of God's presence manifested than to talk to God face to face. What could be more exciting!

Moses was God's friend because he spent time in conversation with the Lord. God drew near to Moses, and Moses drew near to God. They had a mutually rewarding relationship. God enjoyed speaking with Moses. He enjoyed meeting Moses at the Ark of the Covenant.

> *"There I will meet with you, and I will speak with you from above the mercy seat, from between the two cherubim which are on the ark of the Testimony, of all things which I will give you in commandment to the children of Israel."*   Exodus 25:22

God was ready to reveal Himself. He was ready to speak with Moses and to instruct Him. But Moses had to make the effort to approach. He did so because he had a thirst for God's presence. He knew that he could not lead the children of Israel alone. He knew that he was nothing without the Lord's hand upon his life.

> *Then Moses said to Him, "If Your Presence does not go with us, do not bring us up from here. For how then will it be known that Your people and I have*

found grace in Your sight, except You go with us? So we shall be separate, Your people and I, from all the people who are upon the face of the earth."

Exodus 33:15-16

The presence of God was so important to the children of Israel that Moses wanted them to be known as *a people of the Presence*. He wanted them to be recognized as different from all other nations — because they had the presence of the Creator of heaven and earth in their midst, because they had a relationship with their God, because they knew His presence.

The "gods" of the other religions are only idols or men or spirits or principalities. Entering their presence is not enjoyable. You would not want to stay long. Their worship is motivated by fear, not love. God's presence brings rest and peace.

"My Presence will go with you, and I will give you rest."   Exodus 33:14

On one occasion Moses spent forty days in the presence of God (Exodus 24:15-18). His deep relationship with God was unique for his time.

The Lord came down in the pillar of cloud and stood in the door of the tabernacle, and called Aaron and Miriam. And they both went forward. Then He said, "Hear now My words:
If there is a prophet among you,
I, the Lord, make Myself known to him in a vision,

And I speak to him in a dream.
Not so with My servant Moses:
He is faithful in all My house.
I speak with him face to face,
Even plainly, and not in dark sayings;
And he sees the form of the Lord".

Numbers 12:5-8

Moses saw the form of the Lord, His manifest or revealed presence. Not many men walked that close to God. Once, when Moses returned from the presence of God, his face burned with the brilliance of the residue of God's presence (Exodus 34:29).

Moses, though he ran from God at times, had a tremendous longing to be near His Creator and Heavenly Father. On one occasion, He said to God, *"Please, show me Your glory"* (Exodus 33:18).

The Lord responded to his plea:

"I will make all my goodness pass before you.
You cannot see My face; for no man shall see Me, and live.
Here is a place by Me, and you shall stand on the rock. So it shall be, while My glory passes by, that I will put you in the cleft of the rock, and will cover you with My hand while I pass by. Then I will take away My hand, and you shall see My back; but My face shall not be seen."   Exodus 33:19-23

The Lord descended in the cloud and stood with him there, and proclaimed the name of the Lord. And the Lord passed before him.

*So Moses made haste and bowed his head toward the earth, and worshipped. Then he said, "If now I have found grace in Your sight, O Lord let my Lord, I pray, **go among us,** even though we are a stiff-necked people."*   Exodus 34:5-6 & 8-9

Not only did Moses want to be near the Lord; he wanted the people of Israel to experience the presence of God in the same way. Because he spent so much time in God's presence, the Bible says of Moses:

Since then there has not arisen in Israel a prophet like Moses, whom the Lord knew face to face.
                          Deuteronomy 34:10

Have you been living face to face with God? That is His desire for each of His children. He is inviting you to get in His face. Do you have a passion for His presence?

Joshua

After the death of Moses the servant of the Lord, it came to pass that the Lord spoke to Joshua the son of Nun, Moses' assistant, saying:
"As I was with Moses, so I will be with you. I will not leave you nor forsake you .
Do not be afraid, nor be dismayed, for the Lord your God is with you wherever you go.
                          Joshua 1:1, 5-6 & 9

Joshua had the privilege of being an apprentice under Moses, the man who lived face to face with God. As

Joshua grew in his own personal knowledge of God, gradually the mantle of leadership passed to him. Joshua also loved the presence of God. On at least one occasion he stayed behind in the presence of God long after Moses had left.

> *So the Lord spoke to Moses face to face, as a man speaks to his friend. And he would return to the camp, but his servant Joshua the son of Nun, a young man, did not depart from the tabernacle.*
>
> Exodus 33:11

When Moses went up the mountain to meet with God, Joshua was often at his side.

> *Moses arose **with his assistant Joshua,** and Moses went up to the mountain of God.*   Exodus 24:13

On this particular occasion, Joshua waited patiently, for many days and night, as Moses went up further into the cloud of God's manifest presence.

Because he knew God, Joshua became a military genius who brought many victories to Israel. The tactics he employed in conquering the nations of Canaan are still considered classics of military science.

After he had distributed the conquered territory among the tribes, Joshua retired from military life to devote himself to strengthening the worship life of his people. He made this decision at a critical time. Once all their enemies were conquered, most of the people had relaxed their faith and begun to stray from the Lord who saved them (Joshua 24:23-27).

Let us not relax in our quest until we are safely in the ultimate presence of God in eternity.

Gideon

> *The angel of the Lord came and sat down under the oak in Ophrah that belonged to Joash the Abiezrite, where his son Gideon was threshing wheat in a winepress to keep it from the Midianites. When **the angel of the Lord** appeared to Gideon, he said, "**The Lord is with you, mighty warrior.**"*
>
> *"But sir," Gideon replied, "if the Lord is with us, why has all this happened to us? Where are all his wonders that our fathers told us about? ... But now the Lord has abandoned us and put us into the hand of Midian."*
>
> **The Lord turned to him and said, "Go in the strength you have and save Israel out of Midian's hand. Am I not sending you?"**
>
> *"But Lord," Gideon asked, "how can I save Israel? My clan is the weakest in Manasseh, and I am the least in my family."*
>
> **The Lord answered, "I will be with you, and you will strike down the Midianites together."**
>
> Judges 6:11-16 (NIV)

Gideon experienced the manifest presence of the Lord. This *"angel of the Lord"* was a manifestation of the Lord Himself. The Lord appeared and spoke to Gideon, calling him a *"mighty warrior."* Gideon was shocked. He considered himself to be anything but a mighty warrior. As they talked, however, Gideon's attitude changed. The presence and glory of God can change the way you think about yourself too.

If we know that God is with us, we can face all sorts of obstacles. Gideon's confidence was rising, yet he wanted God to give him some sign to assure him that he was not imagining things, that he was really talking to God.

With the tip of the staff that was in his hand, the angel of the Lord touched the sacrifice that Gideon had prepared. Fire flared up from the rock, consuming the offering. At the same time, the *"angel"* disappeared into the smoke. Gideon knew that he had been with God. He exclaimed:

> *"Ah Sovereign Lord! I have seen the angel of the Lord face to face!"*
> *But the Lord said to him, "Peace! Do not be afraid. You are not going to die."*
> *So Gideon built an altar to the Lord there and called it The Lord is Peace.*   Judges 6:22-24 (NIV)

Gideon soon called the men of Israel to battle, defeated the enemies that had been plaguing them for so long, and went on to become one of Israel's renowned judges or rulers. The manifest presence of God changed him from being the *"least"* in his own family to being the greatest and most respected man in all Israel.

Samuel

> *The Lord called Samuel again the third time. Then he arose and went to Eli, and said, "Here I am, for you did call me."*

Then Eli perceived that the Lord had called the boy. Therefore Eli said to Samuel, "Go, lie down; and it shall be, if He calls you, that you must say, 'Speak, Lord, for Your servant hears.' "
*Then **the Lord came and stood and called** as at the other times.*   1 Samuel 3:8-10

Even children can experience the manifest presence of the Lord. Samuel was so young that he didn't understand what was happening to him. He did not yet know the Lord (1 Samuel 3:7). God saw the desire of his heart, came to him, and called him by name.

Samuel had submitted himself to Eli, the priest, and thought that it was Eli who was calling him. Each time, he rose and went to see what Eli wanted. It was Eli who finally realized that God was speaking to a child.

This experience totally changed Samuel's life. Very early he became aware of God's presence with him and learned how to commune with God and to hear His voice. The life-style he thus developed made him such a powerful prophet. During a period when the prophetic word of God was not known, Samuel could boldly speak forth the most profound revelation — because he knew God and heard His voice.

He was a man of God's presence and a man of God's word. The two go together. People of God's presence are also people of His word.

David

As the deer pants for the water brooks,
So pants my soul for You, O God.

My soul thirsts for God, for the living God.
When shall I come and appear before God?
My tears have been my food day and night,
While they continually say to me,
"Where is your God?"   Psalms 42:1-3

David's burning desire for the Lord and His presence took him from the fields and made him Israel's greatest king. Born in 1040 B.C., he was the youngest son of Jesse of Bethlehem. As the youngest son of the family, he was assigned (as soon as he was old enough) to tend the sheep. Required to spend long hours at these duties, David chose to take advantage of the time to get to know God. David loved the Lord very much.

I will love you, O Lord, my strength.   Psalms 18:1

Because he loved the Lord, David was secretly anointed king over Israel at a very young age. He was filled with the Spirit of the Lord, as a young teenager (1 Samuel 16:13).

David learned to play a harp and used it as He sang spontaneous praises to God and developed a relationship with the Creator. Very young he learned of the greatness of Jehovah-Shammah (the Lord who is present), yet he was not afraid to approach God; for he knew God and knew His goodness. He had developed an intimate relationship with Him. So great was David's love for the Lord that his soul ached for the Lord's presence. He was thirsty for God's manifest presence.

Have you been that hungry for the Lord's nearness? Have you been so thirsty for Him that you cried day and night?

David's passion for the Lord's presence did not end when he became king. He honored the Ark of the Covenant, where God's presence dwelled. When the Ark remained for a time in another land (because of an accident that had occurred in the transporting of it), David was not pleased. He could not rest until the Ark was retrieved and brought back to Jerusalem.

> *David consulted with the captains of thousands and hundreds, and with every leader. And David said to all the congregation of Israel, ... "Let us bring the ark of our God back to us.*
> *David and all Israel went up Baalah, to Kirjath Jearim, ... to bring up from there the ark of God the Lord, who dwells between the cherubim, where His name is proclaimed.*   1 Chronicles 13:1-3, & 6

David prepared a special tent where the Ark could dwell safely so that he could have God's presence always near him.

> *David built houses for himself in the City of David; and he prepared a place for the ark of God, and pitched a tent for it.*
> *So it was, when God helped the Levites who bore the ark of the covenant of the Lord, that they offered seven bulls and seven rams.*
> *Thus all Israel **brought up the ark of the covenant of the Lord with shouting and with the sound of***

> *the horn, with trumpets and with cymbals,*
> *making music with stringed instruments and*
> *harps.*
> *So they brought the ark of God, and set it in the midst*
> *of the tabernacle that David had erected for it.*
> *He appointed some of the Levites to minister before the*
> *ark of the Lord.*
>
> 1 Chronicles 15:1, 26, 28, 16:1 & 4

When the people of Israel caught David's vision to bring back the Ark (to bring back the manifest presence of the Lord into their lives), they did it with great celebration. They got noisy. Joyful singing and exuberant praise is still one of the most important ways we can bring the presence of God into our lives.

Most people who believe in the presence of God also believe that this presence can be felt only when and where God chooses. The Bible teaches us, however, that we can experience His presence every time we sing His praises (Psalms 100:2).

David further honored the Ark of the Covenant by writing a dedicatory psalm and permanently installing the ministry of levitical singers under Asaph. His passion for the Lord's presence can be seen in the seventy-three psalms that bear his name. This king was a worshiper. He was constantly praising the Lord. He stimulated Asaph and his associates to the inscriputration of other psalms.

David personally compiled the first psalter or collection of these songs (Psalms 1-41). They are called psalms because of the root word *psalter* which means *harp songs*. Because David often played his harp when he worshiped

in God's presence, his songs of worship are known
a s *psalms.*

The Psalms contain tremendous insights into the presence of the Lord. For example: We can discover how to
enter His presence in Psalm 100. We can find out what
type of praise God likes best in Psalm 22. We can see the
effect *high* praise has on God's enemies in Psalm 149. And
we can learn how various expressions of praise and worship are directly associated with the manifest presence of
the Lord.

Later, David wanted to build a more permanent house
for the Ark of the Covenant.

> *Now it came to pass, as David sat in his house, that
> David said to Nathan the prophet, Lo, I dwell in an
> house of cedars, but the ark of the covenant of the Lord
> remaineth under curtains.*
>
> 1 Chronicles 17:1 (KJV)

David had a burden to honor the Lord by building a
glorious temple for His manifest presence. Although he
was not permitted to build such a temple in his lifetime, he
left explicit instructions for his son Solomon and his aides.

The presence of the Lord made David great.

> *David went on and became great, and the Lord of
> hosts was with him.*   1 Chronicles 11:9

Obed-Edom

> *The ark of God remained with the family of Obed-
> Edom in his house three months. And the Lord blessed*

the house of Obed-edom and all that he had.
1 Chronicles 13:14

During the period when the Ark was absent from Jerusalem, it blessed another family, that of Obed-edom. The circumstances that brought this about were very unusual.

During the reign of Saul, the Ark had been lost in battle with the Philistines. When the presence of God proved to be a curse for the Philistines, they offered to return the Ark. Some men of Judah retrieved it from the enemy but kept it in the home of Abinidab in Kiriath Jearim.

After David had conquered Jerusalem and decided to make it his capital city, he called all the people of Israel from every extremity of the nation to gather and to help bring the Ark of the Covenant on its journey with rejoicing. That must have been a spectacular parade. The Ark rode on a cart pulled by two beautiful oxen. Two chosen men, Uzza and Ahio, drove the oxen and steered the cart as it proceeded slowly along the path toward Jerusalem.

Musicians played harps, other stringed instruments, trumpets, tambourines and cymbals. All the people sang out joyously as they marched forward. It was an idyllic scene.

When they arrived at Chidon, however, something terrible happened to spoil their revelry. The oxen which pulled the cart bearing the Ark stumbled. Uzza put out his hand to steady the ark and was instantly struck dead by the Lord.

David was stunned by this experience. He was both angry and afraid. How could they ever get the Ark back to

Jerusalem if nobody could touch it? He decided to halt the procession and to leave the Ark under the care of some local until he could decide what to do with it. The Ark was taken to the home of a man named Obed-edom. I can imagine how this experience changed the quite life of his family:

Obed-edom and his family are enjoying a quiet meal together at the end of a very busy day, when suddenly there is an intrusive knock at the door. Obed-edom goes to the door and opens it. What he sees startles him.

Before his humble threshold stands a man dressed in complete Levitical attire. Behind him stands a great entourage of people, looking on. Many of the men appear to be musicians. For now Obed-edom doesn't notice the body hanging over one of the donkeys or the presence of the king in the midst of the singers.

"*Yes? May I help you?*" he asks finally.

"*Are you Obed-edom?*" the man asks urgently.

"*Yes, I am,*" he replies, all the while wondering what all this commotion could be about. Why was a group of musicians standing in front of his house? Who was this strange man? And what did they want with him?

"*You see that man standing at the center of the musicians?*" continues the Levite. "*That is King David. And he was wondering if you —* " His voice drops off as if he is having difficulty expressing what is on his mind.

"*Yes?*" prompts Obed-edom, standing on his tiptoes to get a better look at the king.

"*Well,*" said the Levite. "*He wonders if you would mind keeping God for a while. Er — What I mean is that we need to leave the Ark of the Covenant here for a while. Would you mind?"*

Stunned, Obed-edom slowly replies, *"Sure, anything. Well, maybe I had better check with my wife. Could you wait just a moment?"*

He disappears for a moment behind the door and excitedly tells his wife, *"Honey, King David wants to know if we would mind keeping God for a while. It's okay, isn't it?"* Within seconds he re-emerges to state with confidence, *"That would be fine. Put Him right here next to the TV,"* he manages to say.

The Levites bring in the Ark of God in and set it down in the living room, where it will stay for the next three months.

Can you imagine it?

Those were glorious days for the household of Obed-edom! The atmosphere in the home improved immediately when the Ark came through the door.

The children were unusually obedient and courteous. Every day, they did their homework, willingly and cheerfully. When the marking period had passed, they received wonderful report cards.

The wife's garden did very well that spring. Her tomatoes were nearly as large as basketballs. Her watermelons were so large and heavy that one could not be placed on the kitchen table.

The cattle, the donkeys and the sheep all bore young that year. Even the family pet had a litter.

So many things had changed. There was such peace in the household. The TV was rarely turned on now. The family loved to just sit around the living room together in the evenings enjoying the presence of God and of each other. *"And the Lord blessed his household and everything he had."*

When three months had passed, there was another mysterious knock on the door. When Obed-edom opened the door, as was his custom, he found standing there the same Levite who had visited him ninety days earlier. I can just imagine what happened that day:

"Yes? May I help you?" Obed-edom asks.

"Mr. Obed-edom," replies the Levite, *"we have come for God. Is He here?"*

"Yes, He's right there next to the television, where you left Him," is the reply. *"We have immensely enjoyed His presence. Thank you for the privilege of having Him in our house."*

The countenance of the whole family, listening from a safe distance, falls as they hear the news. Obed-edom and his family stand back in hushed silence as the Levites enter the house, insert their long carrying poles into the holy box and take it out the door. As the procession moves off toward Jerusalem, they overhear the people singing, *"We bring the sacrifice of praise into the house of the Lord."*

Long after the sound has died away, they all remain standing, listening, almost afraid to move or speak. Finally Obed-edom makes a move toward the house, and the others follow. The door is shut and the family in silence takes a seat in the living room, each one staring at the space where only a few minutes before the presence of the Lord was.

Things were never the same in the house of Obed-edom again. Something was missing. It almost seemed like someone very close to the family had died. A little later, the book of Kings records the names of the men who were chosen to keep the doors of the house of the Lord. Among them is the name *Obed-edom*. Apparently he had left the farm and moved to Jerusalem with all his family in order to be near the Ark, near to God. This family had grown accustomed to God's presence. Life without Him no longer had any meaning for them.

Have you experienced that same longing for His presence? Does your family want to be near God, to live in His manifest presence? You can. He calls you to His presence. You may have to leave something behind in order to meet Him, but if His presence is important to you, that won't matter. Nothing is more important than His presence.

Satan

Now there was a day when the sons of God came to present themselves before the Lord, and Satan also came among them.   Job 1:6

Satan does not have a passion for God's presence. Quite the contrary! I include him here because he once had the privilege of entering into God's presence — in a heavenly dimension. He lost that privilege. I want to compare his experience with that of redeemed men.

We know that the manifest presence of the Lord constrains and suppresses Satan. When we praise the Lord, He manifests His nearness by repelling spiritual darkness in high places. How is it possible then that Satan could just walk right into the presence of God and carry on a conversation with him?

The Lord said to Satan, "Where have you come from?"
Satan answered the Lord, "From roaming through the earth and going back and forth in it."

Job 2:27 (NIV)

After Satan finished talking with God, the Bible says that *"Satan went out from the presence of the Lord"* (Job 1:12). The same language is used here as in Psalms 100:2 (where the Lord encourages us to come into His presence with singing.) Satan was in that same dimension of God's presence as we now experience. Why? The *Accuser* admitted that he had been out searching for prey. And yet God admitted him into the glory realm. Why?

Jesus, through His death on the cross and His resurrection from the dead, provided for us an entrance into the manifest presence of God. At the same time, He recaptured the keys of death, hell and the grave and, thus, placed definite boundaries upon Satan's activities. Personally, I believe that Satan no longer has access to the reveled presence of God. He can no longer just stroll into the throne room of heaven — when and if he feels like it. The cross marked the beginning of the end for him.

Ezekiel revealed Satan's former position.

"You were in Eden, the garden of God.
You were the anointed Cherub who covers.
I established you.
You were on the holy mountain of God;
You walked back and forth in the midst of fiery stones."   Ezekiel 28:13-14 (NIV)

Most Bible scholars believe that this portion of scripture speaks of Satan before his fall. He was close to God. It is possible that his wings covered the throne of God. He led the heavens in worship to God. *"The holy mountain of God,"* we believe, was the place of worship and sacrifice.

Satan walked in the midst of the stones of fire. These were the celestial luminaries who were in the fire of God's presence. But Satan rebelled against God's authority and tried to exalt himself above his Maker. Because of that, he was removed from the presence of the Lord.

> *I cast you out as a profane thing from the mountain of God, and the guardian cherub drove you out from the midst of the stones of fire. Your heart was proud and lifted up because of your beauty; you corrupted your wisdom for the sake of your splendor. I cast you to the ground.* Ezekiel 28:16-17 (Amplified)

Satan's greatest punishment was to be banished from the presence of Almighty God, to be expelled from His manifest presence. Isaiah also spoke of his fall:

> *How are you fallen from heaven, O light-bringer and day-star, son of the morning! How you are cut down to the ground, you who weakened and laid prostrate the nations. O Blasphemous, Satanic king of Babylon! And you said in your heart, I will ascend to Heaven; I will exalt my throne above the stars of God; I will sit upon the mount of the assembly in the uttermost north;* Isaiah 14:12-13 (Amplified)

Despite his fall, Satan hasn't given us his vile ambitions
— to rule in Zion. His declaration was:

I will sit also upon the mount of the congregation, in
the sides of the north.   Verse 13 (KJV)

We know that this amounted to a declaration of war
with God, for He sat on the sides of the north.

Beautiful for situation, the joy of the whole earth, is
mount Zion, on the sides of the north.   Psalms 48:2

The Church is spiritual Mount Zion:

But you have come to Mount Zion and to the city of
the living God, the heavenly Jerusalem, to an innu-
merable company of angels.   Hebrews 12:22

Satan wants to be the object of our praise, to sit where
God sits, in the praises of His people. *I will sit also upon the*
mount of the congregation. God is sitting there; but Satan
wants to sit there. He wants God's place.

But You are holy, O You Who dwell in [the Holy
Place where] the praises of Israel [are offered].
                         Psalms 22:3 (Amplified)

The word *dwell* here means *to sit or ascend the throne.*
When we praise the Lord, He comes and sits on a throne.
He rules in our midst. I believe that Satan's desire is to sit

in the midst of the worshiping Church. He wants to sit where God sits, where God's throne is. He wants to be restored to the presence of the Lord. Since God will not restore him, he seeks to invade the manifest presence of the Lord as we worship.

At the close of one of our worship seminars in Ohio, a young woman came forward for prayer. When I asked her what her problem was, she told me that during the worship she had experienced a strong desire to strangle her mother (who was worshiping the Lord at her side). It didn't take much discernment to know that we were dealing with the presence of Satan.

The thief comes only to steal and kill and destroy.
John 10:10 (NIV)

That strange compulsion did not come to the young lady before the service, or during the offering, or even during the preaching of the Word. She was influenced by the enemy during the worship time, when God's presence was being manifested. Satan wants to be worshiped too. He wants to sit in God's seat. He wants to rule your life. At the very least, He wants to get some attention.

Resist the enemy and become a person of God's presence, one who has a genuine passion to be with Him.

Chapter 5

The Plan of His Presence

I love those who love me, and those who seek me find me.   Proverbs 8:17 (NIV)

Our heavenly Father longs to be close to His people. He wants to be near those He has chosen and those He loves. He wants to be near YOU. He is partial to you. He loves and cares for you. He not only accepts you but has strong feelings toward you. So strong are those feelings, that He gave His Son to die in your place. It was that act that made it possible for you to get into the proximity of His Person and into the immediacy of His company.

It is a sad thing that Christians can live their entire lives and never experience this kind of intimacy with their heavenly Father. We fill our worship full of religious trappings which distract us from the person of Christ and separate us from His presence. All the while, our Father in heaven desires fellowship, closeness, intimacy, and relationship. He wants us close to Him, at His very bosom.

The Father's ultimate desire is found in the promise of His Word:

For you are the temple of the living God.
"I will dwell in them
And walk among them.
I will be their God,
And they shall be My people."   2 Corinthians 6:16

When John the Revelator saw the new heaven and the new earth appear, and the holy city, New Jerusalem, descending from heaven, he heard a loud voice saying:

"Behold the tabernacle of God is with men, and He
will dwell with them, and they shall be His people, and
God Himself will be with them and be their God.
                                                    Revelation 21:3

His Plan — from the Beginning

This has been His Plan — from the beginning. God created man for fellowship. He enjoyed spending time with Adam — until sin separated God and man, and Adam was driven from the presence of the Creator. Even then, God had a plan to restore man to Himself.

Over the centuries, God worked patiently with the people of Israel to get them to be a nation of priests unto Him. He preserved and guided them through difficult situations so that He could have a unique nation of people who would commune with Him. He said to Moses:

> *"You have seen what I did to the Egyptians, and how I bore you on eagles' wings and brought you to Myself."* Exodus 19:4

God delivered the Hebrew children from Egypt so that they would worship Him. He longed for their fellowship. And today, God desires the same of us.

God will not, however, force His attentions upon us. He is a perfect gentleman. He woos us and calls us, but the final decision is always and completely our own. He anxiously waits for men and women to seek Him.

The Need to Seek God

We are admonished by Scripture to put forth whatever effort is necessary to seek an intimate relationship with our Creator.

> *But if from thence thou shalt seek the Lord thy God, thou shalt find him, if thou seek him with all thy heart and with all thy soul.* Deuteronomy 4:29 (KJV)

> *Now set your heart and your soul to seek the Lord your God.* 1 Chronicles 22:19

These are only a few examples. The need to seek God is one of the major themes of the Bible. The desire of the heart of God is that we actively pursue Him until we find Him. To our God, no biblical principle is more important.

At various junctures of history, Israel's leaders recognized God's plan and actively sought the Lord. They encouraged others to seek Him too.

*Then they [the people of Israel] entered into a covenant
to seek the Lord God of their fathers with all their heart
and with all their soul.*   2 Chronicles 15:12

*And Judah gathered themselves together, to ask help of
the Lord: even out of all the cities of Judah they came to
seek the Lord.*   2 Chronicles 20:4 (KJV)

*And the children of Israel, which were come again out
of captivity, and all such as had separated themselves
unto them from the filthiness of the heathen of the
land, to seek the Lord God of Israel, did eat.*
                                              Ezra 6:21 (KJV)

When we are serious about seeking the Lord, the time
and effort it requires are not important to us. We seek Him
as long as it takes. We put forth whatever effort is
necessary, and we count it a privilege to do so.

Seek the Lord, and his strength: seek his face evermore.
                                              Psalms 105:4 (KJV)

The emphasis here is on continuity. Nothing is more
painful than a temporary relationship. God is looking for
some lasting friendships. Seeking the Lord is not a Sunday
morning pastime. It is a lifelong quest.

During Old Testament times, people living far from the
Temple would make an annual trip to Jerusalem. It seems
like we have a lot of Christians who follow that Old Testament example and only seek God at Christmas or Easter.

But seeking God is something we are to do every day — in our homes, in our offices, in our schools and in our stores. *Seek His face evermore.*

If we love Him, we will continually seek Him until we are, at last, in His ultimate presence in eternity. Even there, we will not stop seeking God. It will remain our priority, our reason for existence.

The ministry of seeking God will never end. It is a fundamental and an ultimate priority. Seeking Him is what we will be doing in heaven forever. Offering Him our worship and adoration will be our only business. We will be fulfilling the first and greatest commandment; loving God with all our heart, soul, mind and strength.

Seeking God is so important that it could have easily been a drive or instinct built into the human being from creation. But God didn't want it that way. He wants the fellowship of caring and loving individuals, so He left us the option of not seeking His presence — just as He left us the option to sin, if we want to sin. He doesn't want to love a bunch of robots. When we decide to seek Him, it means something to Him. It blesses Him. It gives Him happiness. Take the wise option.

The Proper Motivation for Seeking God

Sometimes, the Israelites were motivated by fear or by the problems that invariably beset them when they turned from God. At other times, however, they were motivated by the many promises made in scripture to those who seek the Lord:

*The young lions do lack, and suffer hunger: but they
that seek the Lord shall not want any good thing.*
Psalms 34:10 (KJV)

Seeking the Lord should be a logical goal in life, for He
is the Source of everything that we need.

*Evil men understand not judgement: but they that
seek the Lord understand all things.*
Proverbs 28:5 (KJV)

Tremendous understanding and revelation come to
those who seek the Lord. Answers can be found in His
presence. He is the Source of life and goodness.

Seek the Lord, and ye shall live.   Amos 5:6 (KJV)

*Sow to yourselves in righteousness, reap in mercy;
break up your fallow ground: for it is time to seek the
Lord, till he come and rain righteousness upon you.*
Hosea 10:12 (KJV)

Seeking the Lord effects your spiritual perception. It
gives you an acute awareness of spiritual things. It opens
up to you a whole new world, one of which most of us are
even now unaware.

A life-style of seeking the Lord and spending time with
Him creates broken and contrite hearts that are sensitive
to His ways and wishes. This is God's desire for His
people because it brings us such great benefits. When we

know the benefits that come to those who seek the Lord, we should encourage one another to seek Him in prayer and praise.

We seek Him, however, not just for some benefit that might be derived from being in His presence, not to get answers to some problem we might have at the moment, not just to feel better, and not just to be able to sing a favorite song. We seek Him because we love Him and we love to be near Him.

Some people only pray when they have a need. That is a selfish prayer. Some people use God like some drug to get a "rush" from His presence. That is a selfish motive for seeking Him. Learn to seek God simply for Who He is, to be with Him, to fellowship with Him. Everything else will come. All the many other benefits will be yours.

Just like people of the world, many Christians are asking, "*What is in it for me?*" They can be motivated to prayer and praise only if they are assured that they will "*get something out of it.*" If you are in fellowship with God only for what you can get out of it, you will not develop much of a relationship with Him.

If this is true, you are only seeking God's hand, not His face. You are looking for a handout, not a relationship. When you sit on His lap, don't do it just to give Him your Christmas list, do it to get to know Him better.

So many of our prayers and so much of our worship are self-centered and humanistic. If everything doesn't revolve around us, we're not happy. We are willing to praise God — if it doesn't go on too long. We are not much concerned with what He wants. We are willing to do what is convenient, nothing more.

For example, we are unwilling to move much in our worship if it is too hot in the room. "We" are at the center of our worship and not the Lord. Our desires come first.

The cry of the Holy Spirit today is for His people to dedicate themselves to a serious quest for His manifest presence and to do it for all the right reasons.

> *That they should seek the Lord, if haply they might feel after him, and find him, though he be not far from every one of us.*   Acts 17:27 (KJV)

Do you have a burning desire to draw near to God? Do you have a thirst for Him? Do you have a desire to be where He is? If so, you are willing to pay any price necessary to quench your thirst.

> *But if from thence thou shalt seek the Lord thy God, thou shalt find him, if thou seek him with all thy heart and with all thy soul.*   Deuteronomy 4:29 (KJV)

God is not interested in half-hearted searching. He is calling for intensity in our relationship. It brings Him pleasure to know that people still exist who want to know Him so badly that they will do whatever is necessary to fulfill that longing.

> *Seek the Lord and his strength, seek his face continually.*   1 Chronicles 16:11 (KJV)

When the people of Israel joined together to make a commitment to seek God, they understood that they were making a serious decision. They warned the insincere:

> *That whosoever would not seek the Lord God of Israel*
> *should be put to death, whether small or great,*
> *whether man or woman.*
>
> 2 Chronicles 15:13 (KJV)

That's one way to get people to be serious about seeking God. But our Father in heaven wants those who *willingly* seek Him, not those who seek Him out of obligation, or self-preservation, or any other reason. He wants those who choose to worship Him because they love Him.

The Dangers of Not Seeking God

A great majority of people do not see their need of God. Many of them have more confidence in their own ability to work things out than they do in seeking the Lord for His direction. Their reliance is on something other than the Lord. They would rather take a short cut and deal with things themselves. It seem faster to them. They imagine that they will get quicker results.

They are wrong. The prophet Isaiah warns us:

> *Woe to them that go down to Egypt for help; and stay*
> *on horses, and trust in chariots, because they are*
> *many; and in horsemen, because they are very strong;*
> *but they look not unto the Holy One of Israel, neither*
> *seek the Lord!* Isaiah 31:1 (KJV)

King Rehoboam was not successful. The reason given by the Bible was that *"he prepared not his heart to seek the*

Lord." He was not concerned about knowing the God of
His forefathers.

> *And he did evil, because he prepared not his heart to*
> *seek the Lord.*   2 Chronicles 12:14 (KJV)

The Bible is full of other such sad accounts. Any man or
women who doesn't recognize his/her need of God is
doomed to destruction in this world and the world
to come.

All Men Will One Day Seek Him

God's desire is not just for one nation to seek His presence. It is not just for one special group to come before
Him. His desire is that all the nations seek His presence.
His desire is that the whole world would come before
Him. Despite the rebellious nature of the nations, one day,
according to biblical prophecy, the desire of God's heart
will be fulfilled.

> *And the inhabitants of one city shall go to another,*
> *saying, Let us go speedily to pray before the Lord, and*
> *to seek the Lord of hosts: I will go also. Yea, many*
> *people and strong nations shall come to seek the Lord*
> *of hosts in Jerusalem, and to pray before the Lord.*
> Zechariah 8:21-22 (KJV)

> *But in the last days it shall come to pass, that the*
> *mountain of the house of the Lord shall be established*

in the top of the mountains, and it shall be exalted above the hills; and people shall flow unto it. And many nations shall come, and say, Come, and let us go up to the mountain of the Lord, and to the house of the God of Jacob; and he will teach us of his ways, and we will walk in his paths: for the law shall go forth of Zion, and the word of the Lord from Jerusalem.

Micah 4:1-2 (KJV)

For there shall be a day, that the watchmen upon the mount Ephraim shall cry, Arise ye, and let us go up to Zion unto the Lord our God.   Jeremiah 31:6 (KJV)

Zion is the place of God's presence. There is coming a day when many — from every nation on earth — will go up to Zion and inquire of the presence of the Lord. What a glorious day that will be.

Since the day Adam first sinned, God has had a plan to restore humanity back to Himself. His plan is not just for people to casually make His acquaintance or to be introduced to Him with the hope of getting an invitation to the heavenly party. He wants us to live in constant communion with Him. This is the message of the Gospel; this is the reason God sent His only Son into the world. He came to die for our sins so that we could be the friends of God, once again.

It is not wrong for us to seek to go to heaven to live in His ultimate presence. But unless we learn to live in His presence now, down here, we will not be prepared for heaven later. We don't need to wait until we die. We can experience His presence here now. He is waiting for you to seek Him.

This, then, is the plan of God's presence. He longs to be with His people, to father His family, to have His own, to whom He can be close. This is how His message started in Genesis, the "book of beginnings," and this is how it ends in Revelation, "the apocalypse." This is the theme of the Bible, the heart of the Lord, the plan of His presence. He wants a people with whom He can enjoy continual fellowship.

When we are finally at rest in the presence of our Creator and have the assurance that we need never leave His arms of love, all tears shall cease. In that day, there will be no more separation by death, no more sorrow, no more pain and no more crying. What a wonderful reward that will be for the righteous!

On that day, we will hear the voice of Him Who sits on the Throne. He will say:

> *"Behold, I make all things new."*
> *"He who overcomes shall inherit all things, and I will be His God and he shall be My son."*
>
> Revelation 21:5 & 7

What a day that will be!

Chapter 6

The Privilege, the Prerequisite, and the Passageways

*We have peace with God through our Lord Jesus Christ: By whom also **we have access** by faith into this grace wherein we stand, and rejoice in hope of the glory of God.*   Romans 5:2 (KJV)

This dimension of the manifest presence of God can be experienced by every believer at any time. You don't have to wait until Sunday when the musicians are playing and everyone is singing spontaneous praises. You can enter into His presence at any moment of any day of the year — if you are qualified and if you are willing to learn a few simple secrets.

During all ages, certain men and women have been able to touch God when they needed Him. Those men and women have basked in the sunshine of God's love and have been a blessing and a challenge to others. But this doesn't just happen to some because God is whimsical. There are certain biblical principals which, if properly applied, can lead us into the presence of God.

Like any other door, the portals of heaven can be locked. Only those who learn to unlock them enjoy heaven's delights. Here are a few examples:

Some people keep waiting for revival to come, while others are experiencing revival all the time.

Some people leave the glory when they leave summer camp meeting. They haven't learned to take the glory home with them and live in it day by day.

Some people can't feel God outside of the church building. They haven't learned that He is ready to manifest His presence everywhere, always. We don't have to lose the sense of His presence when the music stops and the musicians go home.

Just as in nature, there is cause and effect with the presence of God. There are prerequisites to entering His glory and there are ways to experience His presence.

The Privilege of His Presence

Although God can sovereignly manifest His nearness to any person at any time, the choice and timing are His. We cannot pick and choose supernatural encounters. He is God. For those of us who are washed in the blood of Jesus and have made Him Lord of our lives, He has given us a special privilege — to come into the Father's presence anytime we choose. What a privilege!

Because of the special relationship we have with God through Jesus, we reap the special benefits of being part of the family of God. What a great honor! This is a greater honor than playing for the President of the United States in the White House or for the Queen of England in Buckingham Palace. Our privilege is to appear before The King of all kings and Lord of all Lords, the Creator of all things.

And He loves it too. He delights in being near His children.

> *The person who has My commands and keeps them is the one who (really) loves Me, and whoever [really] loves Me will be loved by My Father. And I [too] will love him and will show (reveal, manifest) Myself to him — I will let Myself be clearly seen by him and make My self real to him.*
>
> John 14:21 (Amplified)

As we have seen throughout scripture, the cry of the Father is to be with His children. The whole purpose of the Law of Moses was to encourage the people of Israel to approach God.

> *"And on the eighth day he shall take to him two turtledoves, or two young pigeons, and* **come before the Lord,** *to the door of the tabernacle of meeting, and give them to the priest."*   Leviticus 15:14

God's desire, when He spoke through the prophets, was that His people approach Him.

> *When the people of the land shall* **come before the Lord** *in the solemn feasts, he that entereth in by the*

*way of the north gate to worship shall go out by the
way of the south gate.*   Ezekiel 46:9 (KJV)

*Wherewith shall I come **before the Lord,** and bow
myself **before** the high God? shall I come before Him
with burnt offerings, with calves of a year old?*
                                                   Micah 6:6 (KJV)

Although a particular protocol was advised as necessary for approaching God, the emphasis was always on
the need to approach Him, to come near to Him. This is
our privilege.

The Prerequisite to His Presence

The qualification or prerequisite for access into the presence of God is that you know Jesus Christ as your personal
Savior and have been washed by the blood of the Lamb. It
is through His blood that we can enter the Holy of Holies.
It is because of what Christ did on Calvary and in the
tomb that we can approach the Ancient of Days.

*For **through Him** we both have access by one Spirit
unto the Father.*   Ephesians 2:18 (KJV)

Without a personal relationship with Jesus Christ, it is
impossible to draw near to God with the full assurance of
His acceptance. Although He is ever ready to receive
those who want to make Him their Lord and Savior and to
turn their lives around, He said:

> *"I am **the way,** the truth, and the life. No one **comes**
> **to the Father** except through Me."*   John 14:6

In order to have access to the manifest presence of
Father God, it is necessary to have a personal relationship
and regular fellowship with Jesus, as Lord.

> *The Lord is far from the wicked,*
> *But he hears the prayer of the righteous.*
>
> Proverbs 15:29

Because God is everywhere, it seems odd to say that He
is *"far from the wicked."* But in the dimension of His presence that can be felt and appreciated by men, He
withdraws Himself from those who refuse His ways.

The difference between *"wicked"* and *"righteous"* is the
application of the blood of Jesus to our hearts and lives.
We are all wicked, unless and until we have been washed
in the blood of the Lamb and received forgiveness for our
sins. When this takes place, we are no longer outcasts from
the presence of God, and He will draw near to us.

Just as we have no access to salvation apart from Jesus
Christ, and we have no access to heaven apart from Him,
we have no access to worship and His presence that can be
experienced in worship apart from a personal relationship
with God's Son.

He is *"the Way."* He is *"the Truth."* And He is *"the Life."*
When He said, *"No one comes to the Father except through
Me,"* He meant *"no one"* — no matter to which religion he
or she belongs or what merit he or she might have. There

are no exceptions. Christ alone is *"the Way"* to the Father. There is no other way.

> *But Christ came as High Priest of the good thing to come ... . Not with the blood of goats and calves, but with His own blood He entered the Most Holy Place once for all, having obtained eternal redemption.*
> Hebrews 9:11-12

> *Without the shedding of blood there is no forgiveness.*
> Hebrews 9:22 (NIV)

> *This hope we have as an anchor of the soul, both sure and steadfast, and which enters the Presence behind the veil, where the forerunner has entered for us, even Jesus, having be come High Priest forever according to the order of Melchizedek.* Hebrews 6:19-20

> *A better hope is introduced, by which we draw near to God.* Hebrews 7:19 (NIV)

> *For Christ has not entered into the holy places made with hands, ... but into heaven itself, now to appear in the presence of God for us.* Hebrews 9:24 (KJV)

Because of His sacrifice on Calvary, we have the privilege of access beyond the veil of separation which once kept man from the manifest presence of the Father.

> *Therefore, brethren, having boldness to enter the Holiest by the blood of Jesus, by a new and living way which He consecrated for us, through the veil, that is*

> *His flesh, and having a High Priest over the house of God, let us **draw near**, with a true heart in full assurance of faith.* Hebrews 10:19-22

We can draw near to God *"in full assurance."* Our personal relationship to the Father gives us that assurance. His love for us and His promise to be with us gives us this assurance. Every single one of us can have confidence because we know that Christ is with us. We have been *"accepted in the Beloved."*

There is nothing more that we need to do to earn acceptance or favor with God. Jesus did it all. There is nothing more to be done to qualify us to come into His presence. He finished it, making it possible for us to walk right into Fathers presence, look Him in the face, and commune with Him. *"He has made us accepted."* HALLELUJAH!

During a praise and worship service, when God begins to reveal His presence, some Christians feel very unworthy, and that worries them. But I want to assure you that there is nothing to worry about. Feeling unworthiness in the presence of Immaculate Perfection is normal. The prophets had the same feeling. Because we are still human and imperfect, how can we feel totally worthy in God's presence?

This is not cause for alarm. We know that despite our imperfections we are accepted by the Lord. Despite our imperfections, we are loved by the Loveliest. Our loving heavenly Father, who gave us life, is ever present to comfort us in our frailties and to help us overcome every weakness. His presence is not to condemn or punish us, as many have thought.

There is only one prerequisite. If you know Him as your Savior, you have nothing to fear.

The Passageways Into His Presence

There are two basic passageways into God's manifest presence: One is **prayer** and the other is **praise**. They are the twin portals that give us access to Him. David said:

Let my prayer be set forth before thee as incense; and the lifting up of my hands as the evening sacrifice.
Psalms 141:2 (KJV)

Our prayers are like incense from the altar, wafting up before the Lord, ascending before Him, invoking His presence.

And when he had taken the book, the four beasts and four and twenty elders fell down before the Lamb, having every one of them harps, and golden vials full of odours, which are the prayers of saints.
Revelation 5:8 (KJV)

The *"golden vials"* that John saw contain the *"odours"* of prayer. There is an aroma to prayer. Prayer has a smell to it. Those who pray have the smell of heaven on them.

And another angel came and stood at the altar, having a golden censer; and there was given unto him much incense, that he should offer it with the prayers of all saints upon the golden altar which was before the

throne. And the smoke of the incense, which came
with the prayers of the saints, ascended up before God
out of the angel's hand.   Revelation 8:3-4 (KJV)

Prayer is an offering given before the throne of the Lord.
It may be either spoken or sung. In either case, it ascends
before God as incense.

Although God is everywhere, prayer brings us into His
revealed presence. Prayer is associated with God's manifest presence and brings us into a new dimension
with God.

The Lord is far from the wicked: but he heareth the
prayer of the righteous.   Proverbs 15:29 (KJV)

God hears everything. He knows everything. He is everywhere. But He hears the prayer of the righteous in a
special sense. He is near, He is present when the righteous
offer prayers to Him.

For the eyes of the Lord are over the righteous, and his
ears are open unto their prayers: but the face of the
Lord is against them that do evil.
     1 Peter 3:12 (KJV)

The face of the Lord, synonymous with the presence of
the Lord, is *"against them that do evil."* His eyes are *"over the*
righteous." He is present to see and hear us when we pray.

Now therefore, O our God, hear the prayer of thy
servant, and his supplications, and cause thy face to

> *shine upon thy sanctuary that is desolate, for the*
> *Lord's sake.*   Daniel 9:17 (KJV)

Daniel understood that prayer invokes the presence of the Lord. He also experienced the presence of angels when he prayed.

> *Whiles I was speaking in prayer, even the man Gab-*
> *riel, whom I had seen in the vision at the beginning,*
> *being caused to fly swiftly, touched me about the time*
> *of the evening oblation.*   Daniel 9:21 (KJV)

You can enter the presence of the heavenlies at any time in any place, through your sincere prayers to God, the Father.

The second of the twin portals into God's presence is **praise**.

> *Come before His presence with singing.*
> *Enter into His gates with thanksgiving*
> *And His courts with praise.*   Psalms 100:2 & 4

The Hebrew word for thanksgiving here is *towdah*. It means *to lift your hands, as if casting out, as a choir and offer thanks*. The Hebrew word for *praise* in this passage is *tehillah*. It means *to sing spontaneous praise* or *the new song*.

> *He hath put a new song in my mouth, even praise*
> *[tehillah] unto our God: many shall see it, and fear,*
> *and shall trust in the Lord.*   Psalms 40:3 (KJV)

It is not an accident that wherever men sing a new song to the Lord His presence is felt and experienced in unusual ways. This is the praise in which God has declared He dwells.

> *Thou art holy, O Thou that inhabitest the praises* [tehillah] *of Israel.*   Psalms 22:3 (KJV)

When you have learned this wonderful secret of praise, you can come into the presence of the Lord anytime you want to, and anywhere you want to. All you have to do is sing to Him.

Some people, because they think they can't sing very well, feel that they are excluded from even trying to enter God's presence in this way. Surely the Lord would not like the sound of their praise, they reason. They are wrong.

If my two small sons were to come to me and say, "Dad, we have a song for you," I would not reject them. Children sing in their own way. Often they don't sing the proper notes. They sing between the keys. Their tone quality is poor. But I would love it anyway.

Could we imagine a father who would respond: "That's terrible, boys. Don't try to sing to me again until you can sing better"? I can't imagine it. I would want to get close to them and affectionately squeeze them. And that is exactly the response our Heavenly Father has when you sing to Him. He loves it.

God doesn't look on the outward. He doesn't listen to the outward. He looks at the heart; and He listens to the heart. Your voice may be flat, but if your heart if sincere and you are singing to the best of your ability, it is the purest praise.

These two secrets, prayer and praise, are very closely related.

> *Even them will I bring to my holy mountain, and make them joyful in my house of prayer: their burnt offerings and their sacrifices shall be accepted upon mine altar; for mine house shall be called an house of prayer for all people.*   Isaiah 56:7 (KJV)

The Hebrew word for *prayer* here is *tephillah*. This is very close to the word for praise, *tehillah*. The two words are like the two wings of the same bird. They go together. They are the two things that cause us to mount upward into God's presence. Prayer and praise are the only two ways that I am aware of to gain access to the presence of the Lord.

Prayer and praise are to be done continually.

> *Pray **continually**.*   1 Thessalonians 5:17 (NIV)

> *Through Jesus, therefore, let us **continually** offer to God a sacrifice of praise — the fruit of our lips that confess his name.*   Hebrews 13:15 (NIV)

Prayer and praise are meant to be a very strategic part of every Christian's life. Are they an important part of yours? Do you pray continually? Do you continually offer to God a sacrifice of praise?

If Christians would walk with the Lord in a continuum of prayer and praise, they would know the power of God's manifest presence in their lives in a very real way. Try it, and you will be delighted with the results. Don't be surprised when people begin to weep while you are standing in line at the grocery store — because they sense the convicting and yet comforting presence of the Lord in your life.

One day, as a Christian worship team was playing their musical instruments and singing in a public park, they noticed that hardened men began to kneel and cry out to God to help them overcome their sins. Needless to say, that musical team had a life-style of prayer and praise to God. As musicians they had more to offer than simply a lovely song. They had the presence of God with them wherever they went. They had learned to open the passageways into the manifest presence of God.

Chapter 7

The Person of His Presence

I was in the Spirit on the Lords Day, and I heard behind me a loud voice, as of a trumpet.

Revelation 1:10

It is important to distinguish between the outward manifestation of God's presence and His person. During our worship, some of us are guilty of focusing on the manifestations of His presence and not on the Lord Himself. Sensing that He is near — because of what we see or hear or feel — we are tempted to dwell on the obvious and to ignore Him, Whom we cannot see.

The purpose of the manifestation of God's presence is to draw us to Him. When that manifestation becomes the center of our attention, we err and grieve the heart of God.

I enjoy my wife's perfume; but it is my wife that is the object of my attention, not her perfume. In this sense, the presence of God is like the cologne of His person. It catches our attention and makes us know that He is near. But the perfume is not the person. Jesus alone is the object of our adoration.

Man is inherently idolatrous. He will invariably worship something, sometimes anything. As believers, we seek to center man's attention on the Creator of the Universe. He must be the object of our desire. Yet it seems so easy for even true believers to get sidetracked from that focus and to concentrate on things that they can see and hear and touch, rather than on the person of the Divine One.

This is very dangerous. When we are guided by the senses, we can be easily manipulated and misled. Music can move us. Eloquent oratory can move us. Even evil spirits can move us. When, however, our only focus is the person of our God, nothing can move us to error.

Worship God.

> *"The true worshipers will worship the Father in spirit and truth; for the Father is seeking such to worship Him."*   John 4:23

> *"Blessing and honor and glory and power,*
> *Be to Him who sits on the throne,*
> *And to the Lamb, forever and ever."*
>
>   Revelation 5:13

> *Giving thanks always for all things to God the Father in the name of our Lord Jesus Christ.*
>
>   Ephesians 5:20

Since Jesus is God, He is the proper object of our adoration.

> *"I am in the Father and the Father in me."*
>   John 14:11

Even angels are instructed to worship Jesus (Hebrews. 1:6). At His birth, angels worshiped Him with antiphonal singing. In heaven, the elders and the living creatures worship Him (Revelation 4:9-11). We should do the same.

Too much of our praise dwells on what God does for us rather than on Who He is. Because our attention to God often dwells on His provision for us, it can sometimes be carnal. Some of us worship Him because of what we hope to gain from the relationship, not because we love Him.

It is wonderful to praise God for His provisions. But it is more wonderful to praise Him because He is the Provider. It is wonderful to praise Him because He saves us, but it is better to praise Him because He is the Savior. It is wonderful to praise Him because He heals us, but it is better to praise Him because He is the Healer.

Our worship must not be based on need. It is based on our love of His person. Worship the exalted Christ, the Jesus of divine revelation.

When the Lord makes His presence known to us, our immediate response should be to worship Him, not to present our wish list. Knowing God only as the Source of all our needs does not inspire the high praises that He yearns to receive from His people.

When we get married, it is because we have fallen in love with a person, not because we need a cook. Worship to God must be very much like our most intimate expressions of love to each other as husband and wife. We don't talk about the bills that are due in our intimate moments together. That would surely cheapen the expression of our love.

Thanksgiving and praise are often responses to Christ's deeds. Worship, on the other hand, is always based on His person. Worship is one person responding to another person — in love.

The manifestation of God's presence permits us to worship effectively because it enables us to catch a glimpse of the exalted person of Christ. The revelation of His presence lifts our worship to a higher level.

When John the Beloved encountered the presence of Jesus, he first heard a voice. To him, it sounded like a trumpet. It was both loud and authoritative. He heard the voice say:

> *"I am the Alpha and the Omega, the First and the Last," and, "What you see, write in a book and send it to the seven churches which are in Asia."*
> *Then I turned to see the voice that spoke with me.*
>   Revelation 1:11-12

When John heard the voice of the Lord, he turned, expecting to see something. God was real to him. He expected to see God. And because he turned expecting to see, he saw.

> *And having turned I saw seven golden lampstands, and in the midst of the seven lampstands One like the*

*Son of Man, clothed with a garment down to the feet
and girded about the chest with a golden band. His
head and hair were white like wool, as white as snow,
and His eyes like a flame of fire.*   Verses 12-14

What a glorious experience! Most of us would give anything to see what John saw and to hear what John heard. But we imagine that this experience was reserved for a chosen few. We're wrong! I want to tell you that you can have an experience similar to that of John the Revelator — if you are willing to concentrate on the person of Jesus, listen for His voice, and take time to turn to see Him.

If we are willing to seek God as John did, God is ready and willing to reveal Himself to us. Our victorious Champion stands in resplendent glory looking longingly in your direction with those eyes *"like a flame of fire."*

John described Him further:

*His feet were like fine brass, as if refined in a furnace,
and His voice as the sound of many waters:*
                                        Verse 15 (KJV)

There's that *white noise* of heaven again. His voice contains *all the frequencies sounding simultaneously, the combination of all the sound waves in the spectrum that we can hear.* What a voice!

*He had in His right hand seven stars, out of His
mouth went a sharp two-edged sword, and His
countenance was like the sun shining in its strength.*
                                        Verse 16

Can a person look into the sun and not be affected by its brilliance? Jesus' brilliance was as the sun at its brightest. Can anyone look at the Son and not be affected? Of course not. John said:

When I saw Him, I fell at His feet as dead.

Verse 17

This is the appropriate response to the revelation of God's presence. Many people have heard the Lord speak to them; many others have looked to see Him; but few fall prostrate at His feet. John was not forced to fall before the Lord. His heart would not permit him to do otherwise. The heart of a true worshiper finds only one appropriate expression, that of total prostration; for the glory of God's presence causes a mixture of gut-wrenching fear and profound worship.

He laid His right hand on me, saying to me, "Do not be afraid; I am the First and the Last. I am He who lives, and was dead, and behold, I am alive forevermore. Amen. And I have the keys of Hades and of Death."   Verse 17-18

John was seeing the absolute and total Victor, He Who has triumphed from the beginning of history and Who will continue to triumph till the end of time. This was His Eminence, the Eternal One. Praise be to our God forever and ever! When John saw Him, he fell down as if he were dead. We should all bow low in His presence.

This is the revelation of the Person of our worship. He is the Center of our exaltation. He is the Focus of our adoration and reference. He is the Recipient of all honor and praise. He is the One we love so dearly. Therefore we burn with a passion to be near Him. We have **a passion for His presence**.

While He was on the earth, Jesus was the presence of the Father incarnate, the very presence of God embodied, made manifest, *"made flesh,"* the Divine mixed with the human.

> *The Word [Christ] became flesh (human, incarnate) and tabernacled — fixed His tent of flesh, lived awhile — among us; and we [actually] saw His glory — His honor, His majesty.*   John 1:14 (Amplified)

Let Him become the object of your own worship, and teach others to concentrate on Him too.

When worship leaders in every culture stand before their respective congregations and endeavor to lead the people into God's presence, they may be challenged with these biblical words:

> *"Sir, we wish to see Jesus."*   John 12:21

It is not an emotion or a feeling that we personally seek, and to which we seek to lead others. It is the person of the exalted Christ and the manifestation of His person. Develop a passion for His presence.

Chapter 8

The Witness of His Presence

For we do not wrestle against flesh and blood, but against principalities, against powers, against the rulers of the darkness of this age, against spiritual hosts of wickedness in the heavenly places.

Ephesians 6:11-12

Four Christian musicians from the United States were playing for the worship service of a church in a resort town in Mexico. The sermon had just ended, and the minister encouraged everyone to praise the Lord together. The worship team led out in songs in Spanish, and the congregation joined them.

After they have praised together for a while, there was an unusual sense that God was very near. People began to come forward and present themselves to the Lord. Some were believers from the local church; but many others were visitors from the neighborhood. All of them were responding to an unseen supernatural force which was drawing them to the front.

Christians began to encircle those who had come forward to be prayed for. After about twenty minutes of prayer, one of the ladies who had come for prayer got down on her hands and knees and began to crawl, hissing like a cat. The Christians prayed with more fervor, while the musical team continued praising the Lord.

Hissing loudly, the woman tried to crawl away from those who were ministering to her in prayer.

What a strange scene! It raises some serious questions:

What was happening in this service?
Why was this woman behaving in this irrational way?

The power of God's presence in praise and worship disturbs the spirit world. The demons in this woman revealed themselves and controlled her body, making her act like an animal. It didn't happen during the preaching or during the offering, but during the time of praise and worship and prayer.

This strange scene actually happened and is a witness to the fact that God inhabits the praises of His people. When we sing our worship to Him, we can expect to experience His presence in very real ways.

There is an increasing awareness among believers of the witness that occurs in worship. When the Lord reveals Himself in the midst of the worship of His people, He provides a witness, a testimony of His glory. This witness takes three forms. First, there is a witness to the spirit world — the kingdom of darkness. Secondly, there is a witness to the unbeliever. And thirdly, there is a witness to the believer.

The Witness to the Spirit World

Dr. Sam Sasser, the man who was used of God to help me understand the new song, once told me about an experience he had as a missionary in the Marshal Islands. When he was on the island of Yap in the Eastern Caroline Islands, he was challenged by an old village chief, who wanted to prove that his traditional god was greater than this new-fangled God that Dr. Sasser preached. He confronted Dr. Sasser in a public meeting where some thirty men were sitting on the ground in a circle.

"The god that we serve is ten times stronger than anything you have ever seen," the chief declared boldly.

"You are wrong," Dr. Sasser answered.

The chief said, "I'll prove it," whereupon he began clapping his hands in a tribal rhythm. The other men joined him. Two women entered the circle and began dancing with their hands raised. Soon the women rose ten feet into the air, held up by the evil forces that had ruled the tribe for so long.

"What do you think about that?" the chief asked. "Would you like to join them? Can you do it?"

"I can do better than that," Dr. Sasser replied. "I can bring them down!"

The chief was not convinced. "Just try it," he dared.

Dr. Sasser began to sing a new song of worship to Jesus. Within ten seconds both the women fell to the ground.

The men who sat in the circle, obviously spirit mediums, were amazed, and the presence of God had a powerful witness in that place. It didn't take thirty Christians, just one worshiper who knew how to touch God's presence. God inhabits the praises of His people — as we have seen.

The manifestation of God's presence through worship broke the hold the spirits had on these women's bodies. The two ladies who danced and who had been lifted into the air by demons were hurt when they fell. When Dr. Sasser prayed for them, however, they were miraculously healed.

The power of God's manifest presence has the authority to drive out darkness in the atmosphere. We have nothing to fear.

> *Be strong in the Lord and in the power of His might.*
> *Put on the whole armor of God, that you may be able*
> *to stand against the wiles of the devil.*
>
> Ephesians 6:10

Our battle is with the rulers of the darkness that are in the atmosphere over cities and other key geographical locations. Demons, or spirits, dwell in areas where there are concentrations of people. Their purpose is to influence, (oppress or possess) human beings. The rulers or kings (fallen angels) govern this chaotic world of demons.

The Bible associates the kings of the darkness of this world with geography. The *"prince of Persia"* was a principality over Persia in the time of Daniel (Daniel 10:13). This was an invisible creature of darkness or fallen angel that resisted Gabriel when he was bringing an answer to Daniel's prayer. Michael, the mighty warring Cherub, came to help Gabriel oppose the prince of Persia. And, after twenty-one days, his opposition was overcome.

When the Lord inhabits the praises of His people, His presence is a deterrent to the powers of darkness. His manifest presence witnesses to His power, to the work Christ did at Calvary, and to the empty tomb He left when He rose from the dead and made possible our new life in Him.

Christ has *"disarmed principalities and powers"* (Colossians 2:15). He stripped Satan of his power and authority and left him with a hollow kingdom of darkness. The King James Version of the Bible uses the word *"spoiled."*

And having spoiled principalities and powers, he made a shew of them openly, triumphing over them.

The word *spoil* used here means *to strip and stuff a kill.* Jesus is the Master Taxidermist. He has stripped and stuffed the Devil.

Taxidermy is an art. First, the dead animal's insides are removed, then the skin is stuffed. Finally, false eyes and a tongue are inserted to make the stuffed animal look lifelike. That is exactly what Christ has done to our enemies.

He made a public spectacle of them, triumphing over them.

Jesus made a public demonstration, a noisy, proclamatory parade over the fallen state of the enemy. Thus He gave witness to the spirit world of His power and presence.

When we worship the Lord, His presence is there to witness of His resurrection power. His presence reminds the kingdom of darkness and its chief of their total lack of power against our God and against His people. Our enemies are impotent in the sight of God.

That is why the spirit world gets restless when we begin to worship. Demons go on "red alert" and man their battle stations. All sorts of alarms go off, and those who are influenced by demonic power begin to act irrationally.

Demons don't mind our being religious. They are religious themselves. They just don't want us to worship God in spirit and in truth; for when that happens, Jesus shows up. His manifest nearness renders useless all the powers of darkness.

This revelation is causing entire congregations to arise and march through the streets of their cities to put the powers of darkness on notice that we intend to take back all that Satan has stolen.

The Lord inhabits His church and His church is charging the gates (meaning the power and authority) of hell. As we go forth to battle, Jesus is with us. As Israel carried the Ark of the Covenant into battle, so we carry the presence of the Lord in our worship. With His help, we can storm the very gates of hell.

In the "Epistle to the Ephesians," Ignatius of Antioch, who died in 110 A.D. wrote: *Take heed, then, often to come together to give thanks to God, and show forth His praise. For when ye come frequently together in the same place, the powers of Satan are destroyed, and his "fiery darts" urging to sin, fall back ineffectual. For your concord and harmonious faith prove his destruction, and the torment of his assistants.* [1]

The presence of God in our corporate worship displaces the power of the enemy in our minds and in the atmosphere. Our worship torments the powers of darkness because it brings the manifestation of the presence of Almighty God.

> *The manifold wisdom of God might be made known by the church to the principalities and powers in the heavenly places, according to the eternal purpose which He accomplished in Christ Jesus our Lord, in whom we have boldness and access with confidence through faith in Him.*   Ephesians 3:10-12

Never underestimate the significance of the witness of God's manifest presence to the powers in the heavens. Satan doesn't underestimate it. He knows that when the Church really gets serious about worshiping God, his territory is under attack; and he is in danger of losing some of his spoils.

The Witness to the Unbeliever

An American missionary in Japan tells how the presence of God in Christian worship affected an unbelieving couple: *The congregational singing that morning at Living Way Church in the city of Shizuoka, southeast of Tokyo, was*

---

1. (The Ante-Nicene Fathers, Vol. 1, Grand Rapids:W.B. Erdmans, p.55)

particularly enthusiastic and God's presence was nearly tangible. After the meeting, the two visitors approached one of the leaders with a sense of wonder. "When you were singing those songs," they said, "we felt a 'presence.' Was that God?" [2]

The leader explained to them that they were experiencing a fulfillment of that Old Testament promise that God inhabits the praises of His people. He went on to tell them about Jesus Christ. His words were weighty, for they had felt the witness of God's presence before he spoke.

When the Church gathers to worship, it gathers to witness. That is one of the reasons we worship publicly — to witness to the unbeliever of the power of our God.

Jesus said that the Son of Man came into the world *"to seek and to save that which was lost"* (Luke 19:10). He also came to seek true worshipers.

> *For the Father is seeking such to worship Him.*
> John 4:23

The Father sent Christ to seek and save us for the specific purpose of providing a worshiping people. The presence of God in our worship will witness to those unbelievers who are present that the Father is drawing them by His Spirit, as well.

There is a relationship between the presence of God in our "up-reach" in worship and our "outreach" in evangelism. Worship is the goal of our evangelism, and evangelism is the natural fruit of our worship.

---

2. (From a Worship Evangelism article by Gerrit Gustafson, **Charisma Magazine,** October 1991)

Unbelievers receive a witness of the presence of God when we worship. They give their lives to Christ and are discipled as worshipers themselves. As they worship, others will receive the witness of Christ, and the cycle will continue.

True evangelism produces worshipers. And true worshipers want to bring others into God's presence; so they evangelize. The two are not mutually exclusive, but mutually inclusive.

Most evangelism is motivated by guilt and obligation. And those who are won are often introduced to an incomplete theology, void of an understanding of worship. True evangelism is born of a loving and worshiping heart. Worshipers burn with a passion to see others experience God's presence.

Without a sense of world mission and the passion that the Father has to *"seek"* others to be worshipers, our worship can become self-serving, as we look for only the "rush" that comes from being in His presence.

Worship has an evangelistic effect for the same reason that demons get nervous when we praise God, because God manifests His presence through worship. And that makes all the difference in the world!

> *"He who sacrifices thank offerings honors me, and he prepares the way so that I may show him the salvation of God."*　　　　　Psalms 50:23 (NIV)

God's presence brings the conviction of sin that must always precede conversion. Wherever the living presence of Jesus is manifested, one of two things happens. Either men and women fall down and confess their sins or they run away and hide from the presence of God.

David Wilkerson, who now pastors a church in Times Square, reported: *During one Tuesday night service at Times Square Church, I was overwhelmed as the presence of Jesus became manifest through the godly worshipers waiting upon Him. People came to the altar, some weeping. The fear of the Lord was awesome. I felt like Isaiah who said "Woe is me! for I ... am a man of unclean lips and I dwell in the midst of a people of unclean lips" (Isaiah 6:5). The presence of Jesus has power to destroy and drive out sin!*

The Psalmist declared:

> *Let God arise,*
> *Let his enemies be scattered:*
> *Let those also that hate him flee before him.*
> *As smoke is driven away,*
> *So drive them away:*
> *As wax melts before the fire,*
> *So let the wicked perish at the presence of God.*

Psalms 68:1-2

Wickedness cannot stand in the presence of God Almighty. It must wither in His glory. The demonic strongholds that Satan has in many people's lives are dissipated when those people come into the presence of the Lord. The manifestation of God's glory frees them to make a decision to permanently come out from under the influence of the enemy and live in the glow of God's goodness.

Not every unbeliever responds.

> *"Then you will begin to say, 'We ate and drank in Your presence, and You taught in our streets.'*
> *But He will say, 'I tell you I do not know you, where you are from. Depart from Me, all you workers of iniquity.' "* Luke 13:26-27

Some sinners seem to take delight in the fact that can sit in the presence of the Lord and yet remained unchanged. They resolve to remain firm and to be unaffected by God's glory. They sit among the saints who's faces glow with the glory of His presence, yet they are not moved to righteousness. God cannot violate the free will with which He endowed every man. He is powerless to change the minds of those who are determined to remain closed to His will and way.

On September 15th, 1990, more than two hundred thousand Christians filled the streets of cities all across Great Britain. They marched in unison, shouting slogans, brandishing placards and singing with enthusiasm. On that day, believers in Great Britain took their worship into the streets and left a lasting witness to unbelievers.

In March of 1991, in Austin, Texas, one hundred and fifty thousand Christians from one hundred and twenty churches marched through the streets of the capitol invoking the presence of Jesus in prayer and praise. Similar public displays of worship have been seen in Australia, South Africa, Germany, Holland, Japan, Canada, Singapore and other countries.

Says Graham Kendrick, one of the organizers of these marches: *It is based on a very simple principle of taking the Church to the streets, giving glory to God, praying for His kingdom to come and His will to be done.*

Graham finds the motivation for such activities in sacred Scripture:

> *Oh, give thanks to the Lord!*
> *Call upon His name;*
> *Make known His deeds among the peoples!*
> *Sing to Him, sing psalms to Him;*
> *Talk of all His wondrous works.*

Psalms 105:1-2

On the Day of Pentecost, when the Holy Spirit fell on one hundred and twenty followers of Christ, those newly filled believers spilled out into the street and began openly praising God. The people of the community heard the commotion and gathered to ask: *"What is this?"* (Acts 2:12). After Peter explained what was happening, three thousand people gave their lives to Christ. Worship results in the presence of Jesus revealed. And when worship is public, the witness of His presence is for everyone to behold.

People are no longer asking, "What is this?" One reason is that so much of what the church does occurs behind closed doors. We are very protective of our privacy in worship. As a result, our worship presents very little witness to the unbeliever. Sinners are forced to enter a building where Christians regularly worship in order to experience the presence of the Lord. And the once powerful and visible Church is nearly invisible, as a result.

In recent years, the Holy Spirit is calling the Church back to public worship, calling us back to praise God *"among the heathen."*

> *All Your works shall praise You, O Lord,*
> *And Your saints shall bless You.*
> *They shall speak of the glory of Your kingdom,*
> *And talk of Your power,*
> *To make known to the sons of men His mighty acts,*
> *And the glorious majesty of His kingdom.*
>
> Psalms 145:10-12

The Scriptures challenge us:

> *You are a chosen generation, a royal priesthood, a holy*
> *nation, His own special people, that you may proclaim*
> *the praises of Him who called you out of darkness into*
> *His marvelous light;*   1 Peter 2:9

The Christians of the early centuries experienced the witness of God's presence in their public worship. Polycarp wrote of Christ's manifest presence bringing Romans to repentance in the arenas of Rome. The hearts of the believers were broken for the loss of the Christians being led into the arenas to be fed to the dogs and lions. When the bars were released and the condemned believers were forced into the open in front of the screaming crowd, they sang praises to God. Unashamedly and with a loud voice, they sang spontaneous praise by the Spirit as they marched to their death.

Because of this public display of worship and faith, Polycarp reported, hundreds of Roman spectators cried out in repentance to God. The power of God's presence in the martyrs' praise changed the atmosphere for some of the spectators of this blood sport. What greater witness could the Romans have received? It was this convincing presence of Jesus that made the Church grow mightily in the first century. Nearly two millennia later, the revealed presence of the Lord Jesus Christ is still the key element of convincing demonstration to the lost. Oh, how we need the power of the manifest presence of Jesus to convince the world of sin and to cause the Church to grow mightily in the coming days!

The Witness to the Believer

The manifestation of the Lord's presence witnesses to the Christian in several ways. One way is the sense of endearment. This is often felt by believers, especially during participation in the "Eucharist" or holy communion, observed regularly by large numbers of believers all over the world.

> *For we being many are one bread, and one body: for we all partakers of that one bread.*
> 1 Corinthians 10:17 (KJV)

When we meet at the table of the Lord, there is a special sense of unity among brothers, a sense of true equality, a sense of God's love to each of us and to all of us. It is a joyous occasion and a solemn occasion. In this great mystery of God's love for each of us, we see His love and beauty manifested and are drawn to Him. We receive a revelation, an awareness of Who the Lord is. We become more conscience of His nature. And it changes us.

We all, with unveiled face, beholding as in a mirror the glory of the Lord, are being transformed into the same image from glory to glory, just as by the Spirit of the Lord.   2 Corinthians 3:18

When we, as believers, behold the manifest presence of the Lord, we change. And the longer we remain in His presence the further along we move in this process of changing into His image. The manifestation of His presence with us is a witness of His love for us.

His presence also convicts believers of sin. In the presence of Him Who is sinless, we become conscious of wrong attitudes and wrong behavior. The closer we get to His presence, the more we see the imperfections in our lives and are able to deal with them.

The Scriptures admonish us:

"Repent therefore and be converted, that your sins may be blotted out, so that times of refreshing may come from the presence of the Lord."   Acts 3:19

The witness of Christ's revealed presence is convincing and convicting. It will not leave us unchanged, but ever draws us closer to His perfect image.

Chapter 9

The Challenge of His Presence

As the hart pants and longs for the water brooks so I pant and long for You, O God. My inner self thirsts for God, for the living God. When shall I come and behold the face of God? My tears have been my food day and night, while men say to me all the day long, Where is your God? Psalms 42:1-3 (Amplified)

Do you have that kind of passion for the Lord's presence, an intense desire to get close to Him, to experience His manifest presence? Would you like to have it?

Sometimes our spiritual desire is sporadic. When was the last time you were really thirsty for the Lord's presence? Was it at youth camp three years ago? Or in church that Sunday last year when that guest evangelist came and you went to the altar at the front of the church to let God know you were serious about Him? Or has it been even longer?

How about now? Are you thirsty for God's presence right now? Do you want to live in His presence and walk in His presence? How would your desire rank among your top five priorities in life?

David said:

> *One thing have I asked of the Lord, that will I seek after, inquire for and [insistently] require, that I may dwell in the house of the Lord [in His presence] all the days of my life, to behold and gaze upon the beauty [the sweet attractiveness and the delightful loveliness] of the Lord.*   Psalms 27:4 (Amplified)

Do you feel distant from God? Do you sense a separation between His presence and yourself? Have you withdrawn yourself from Him for some reason? Or do you even feel totally cut off from the Lord, removed, severed and faraway from His presence?

If so, are you satisfied to stay that way? Are you satisfied to live in that state? The Lord is calling you today.

> *You have said, seek you My face — inquire for and require My presence [as your vital need]. My heart says to You Your face [Your presence], Lord will I seek, inquire for and require [of necessity and on the authority of Your Word].*
> *Hide not Your face from me; turn not Your servant away in anger, You have been my help! Cast me not off.*   Psalms 27:8-9 (Amplified)

You do not need to feel distant from the Lord anymore. He has made it clear in His Word that His desire is for you to live in His manifest presence. He has provided a way for you to come into His presence and to get close to Him. And He has shown you the methods of approaching Him anytime, any where — at will. He is calling you now. Come close to God, and He will come close to you (See James 4:8).

It is your move. God has done everything possible to insure your fellowship with Him. Now, He awaits your decision. He is anxiously watching to see if you will come to Him. Don't disappoint Him.

Take that first step now. And don't let it be the last. I challenge you to develop a passion for the manifest presence of the Lord. Let His presence be your highest request and your greatest need. And may all other things become secondary in your life.

If you don't have this infatuation for God's presence, you can acquire it. Begin a diligent and consistent personal devotional time with the Lord. Let it be a time to read His Word, to pray, and to praise Him. As you get to know Him, your love will grow. Before long, you will have a passion for His presence.

If reading the Bible is a chore for you, try doing it out loud for a while. Hearing your own words will enable you to develop an appetite for our Lord and His manifest presence.

Don't be rushed. Take time to focus on Him and to express your desires to Him fully. You don't have anything more important to do. Allow a God-consciousness to slowly seep into your soul. After a while you will look forward to these times alone with the Lord, as David did.

If this is your desire, I want to lead you in prayer. Please pray with me as you read these words. Say them from your heart.

Gracious Heavenly Father,
I have made my decision to draw near to You in worship and to search for Your presence.

Deliver me from seeking an "experience." Help me to seek Your face and to develop a hunger for Your presence. Let Your nearness in my life be my most ardent affection.

Forgive me for having other desires (god's) before You. Cleanse my spirit of lethargy and indifference. Deliver me from the routine of worship, from "business as usual," from form without force and liturgy without life.

May Your Holy Spirit energize the "new creation" that is in me to worship You with spirit and in reality. Make my worship whole-hearted, warm and vibrant. Remind me, whenever necessary, that the "door of praise" is always open for me to come into Your revealed presence. I make You my quest and my infatuation. You are my love and my life. To You I give all my affection today and always.

In the name of Jesus,

Amen!

Bibliography

1. Charnock, Stephen. *Existence and Attributes of God*, Grand Rapids, MI: Baker Book House, 1987
2. Warren W. Wiersbe, *Real Worship*, Nashville, TN, Oliver Nelson, 1986
3. Jack Hayford, *Worship His Majesty*, Waco, TX, Word Books, 1987
4. John MacArthur, Jr., *The Ultimate Priority*, Chicago, IL, Moody Press, 1983
5. Judson Cornwall, *Let Us Draw Near*, South Plainfield, NJ, Logos, 1977
6. Judson Cornwall, *Elements of Worship*, South Plainfield, NJ, Logos, 1985
7. Judson Cornwall, *Let Us Worship*, South Plainfield, NJ, Logos, 1983

Audio Tapes by LaMar Boschman

001 The Call and Function of a Worship Leader
002 The Priority of Worship
003 The Goals of a Worship Service
004 Establishing Continuity in Worship
005 Developing the Life-style of a Worshiper
006 Leading Worship in the 90's
007 The Ultimate Priority
008 The Role of Men in Worship
009 How to Improve Congregational Involvement
010 Principles of Leading Worship
011 The Role of the Musician in the Kingdom
012 The Worship Leading Team
013 How to Lead Worship Under the Direction of the Holy Spirit
014 Praise and Worship: What's the Difference?
015 The Pastor's Role in Worship
016 The Lord of Hosts in Battle

(Each tape is $4. Please add $2 for shipping and handling.)

Send to:
LaMar Boschman Ministries
P.O. Box 130
Bedford, TX 76095

International Worship Leaders' Institute

Now you can get the concentrated, intensive training you desire. The International Worship Leaders' Institute, a training school for church leaders: including pastors, worship leaders, instrumentalists and singers, is conducted in Dallas, Texas.

The Institute staff is specifically chosen because of their wealth of knowledge and area of expertise to provide a thorough and well-balanced curriculum. You will receive five days of extensive classroom instruction and small group discussions, a three-ring study guide, practical helps and suggestions, and a graduation certificate.

Our mission is to help train and equip worship leaders, pastors, instrumentalists, singers and worship teams from around the world so that they can be more effective in leading others into the presence of the Lord. This is one of the greatest opportunities available to worship teams today.

For more information, please write:

International Worship Leaders' Institute
P.O. Box 130
Bedford, TX 76095

THE REBIRTH OF MUSIC
NOW IN ITS 9TH PRINTING—
Introduction by Phil Driscoll

In LaMar's best-selling book, you'll learn how your music can be filled with the power and presence of the Holy Spirit. Through years of ministering to worship leaders, singers, musicians, and churches, LaMar has gained many practical insights into the real meaning and purpose of music. You'll also gain a solid biblical perspective through 989 scripture references to music. Retail $5.95
Also available in Spanish. Retail $5.95

THE PROPHETIC SONG
Foreword by Judson Cornwall

In this exciting book, LaMar helps you understand and experience the prophetic song God is restoring to the church. You'll experience new victories and enter new heights of worship as you learn to prophecy with instruments and with singing. All Christians are called to sing a new song. Retail $4.95

THREE COMPLETE SEMINARS ON AUDIO AND VIDEO TAPE!

At last, Church music departments can hold their own training seminars on Praise and Worship! A 40-page syllabus of notes and quizzes for group meetings or individual study can be ordered separately.

LaMar answers questions about the relevance and importance of music in the church today, the musician's true function in God's kingdom and much more. You'll catch excitement of a vision for worship with the "live" format of these tapes. This series is a must for all church music departments.

Local Church Worship Seminar #1	Local Church Worship Seminar #2	Local Church Worship Seminar #3
Videos (90 min. each) Set of 3—$99 ($39.95 each)	**Videos** (90 min. each) Set of 3—$99 ($39.95 each)	**Videos** (90 min. each) Set of 3—$99 ($39.95 each)
Video #1 Genesis of Music/ Satan and Music **Video #2** The Songs that Kill/ Goals of a Worship Service **Video #3** The Role of the Musician/The Importance of Music	**Video#1** Expressions of Worship and Warfare/ Definitions of Praise **Video #2** Plowing with Praise/ Praise in the Life of Jesus **Video #3** The Role of Music in the Prophetic Song/ What is True Worship?	**Video #1** The Ultimate Priority!/ Role of Men in Worship **Video #2** Which Music is of God?/ The Worship Leading Team **Video #3** Banners and Processionals/Prophecy in the Prophetic Song
Six-tape Audio Cassette Series—$25	**Six-tape Audio Cassette Series—$25**	**Six-tape Audio Cassette Series—$25**

SYLLABUS—$4.95 (10 or more 10% discount)
Seminar outlines and quizzes for each section. Excellent study material for individual as well as group settings.

20% off if you order all three videos or all three audio tapes

EXALTATION

It's new and it's powerful! Ten dynamic songs on the exaltation and preeminence of Christ. This solo album by LaMar Boschman has a wide variety of musical styles, from soft ballad, jazz, gospel, to "rap" like on "Army of God." Other songs include "Let's Glorify Jesus," "I Shall Rise," "There Is a Way," "Worship the Lord," "All Over the World," "Take Me In," and "Father's Heart." Retail $8.98

GIVE UNTO THE LORD

A very *live* worship tape recorded at the International Worship Leaders' Institute in Dallas, Texas. This tape includes many upbeat praise songs as well as intimate songs of worship—all in a contemporary style. Some of the songs include: "Glory to the King," "Celebrate Jesus," Carman's "Lord of All," "Come Let Us Sing for Joy," "I Will Sing," and "Commune With Me." It also contains a prophetic reading out of Revelation and spontaneous praise. Retail $8.98